God bless you!

WHAT NO
EYE HAS SEEN

WHAT NO EYE HAS SEEN

Why We All Should Look Forward to Heaven

Charles K. Stanley

WESTBOW
PRESS
A DIVISION OF THOMAS NELSON

All scripture quotations, unless otherwise indicated, are taken from the Holy Bible, New International Version®, NIV®. Copyright ©1973, 1978, 1984, 2011 by Biblica, Inc.™ Used by permission of Zondervan. All rights reserved worldwide. www. zondervan.com. The "NIV" and "New International Version" are trademarks registered in the United States Patent and Trademark Office by Biblica, Inc.™

Scripture quotations marked (MESS) are taken from the Message®, Copyright © 1993, 1994, 1995, 1996, 2000, 2001, 2002 by Eugene H. Peterson.

Scripture quotations marked (KJV) are from the Holy Bible, King James Version, public domain.

Scripture quotations marked (AMP) are taken from the Amplified Bible, Copyright © 1954, 1958, 1962, 1964, 1965, 1987 by The Lockman Foundation. Used by permission.

Scripture quotations marked (NLT) are taken from the Holy Bible, New Living Translation, copyright © 1996, 2004, 2007 by Tyndale House Foundation. Used by permission of Tyndale House Publishers, Inc., Carol Stream, Illinois 60188. All rights reserved.

WestBow Press books may be ordered through booksellers or by contacting:

WestBow Press
A Division of Thomas Nelson
1663 Liberty Drive
Bloomington, IN 47403
www.westbowpress.com
1-(866) 928-1240

Because of the dynamic nature of the Internet, any web addresses or links contained in this book may have changed since publication and may no longer be valid. The views expressed in this work are solely those of the author and do not necessarily reflect the views of the publisher, and the publisher hereby disclaims any responsibility for them.

Any people depicted in stock imagery provided by Thinkstock are models, and such images are being used for illustrative purposes only.

Certain stock imagery © Thinkstock.

ISBN: 978-1-4908-0479-8 (sc)
ISBN: 978-1-4908-0480-4 (hc)
ISBN: 978-1-4908-0478-1 (e)

Library of Congress Control Number: 2013914487

Printed in the United States of America.

WestBow Press rev. date: 08/19/2013

What no eye has seen,
what no ear has heard,
and what no human mind has conceived—
the things God has prepared for those who love him.

—Paul the Apostle of Jesus Christ, 1 Corinthians 2:9 (NIV)

To Leah, Nathan, and Rebecca
For making me the proudest father on earth

And to Diane
For making me the happiest man.

Contents

Introduction
Our Future in Heaven

I was a new pastor assigned to my first church. Ruth, who introduced herself as the church's Sunday School superintendent, visited in my office to tell me about why her friend Angie stopped coming to church. I braced myself to hear what I thought would be typical complaints about the church. Instead, Ruth told me a story of profound loss and grief.

She said that Angie was, at one time, very active in the church, and even taught a Sunday School class. But Angie had dropped out in the past year, following a tragic loss—the birth of a stillborn child. Ruth asked me if I might visit Angie sometime. I told her I would.

Several weeks later, I was visiting our most aged members and the elder care facility in the town where Angie lived. The weather bureau had predicted a midday snowstorm, so I finished my visits early and left, hoping to get home before the snow hit.

As I drove south on the highway that led back home, I passed the road where Angie lived, which I had passed on all my trips to Cedar Springs. But on this occasion, as I passed by the intersection, an inner voice spoke; a voice that was both urgent and insistent. It said, "Go see Angie, now."

Hoping that voice was my own, I drove on. But the voice kept insisting, "Go see Angie, now!" the further away I got from Angie's home, the more urgent that voice became. Eventually, I performed a U-turn and went back to the intersection and turned onto Angie's road.

A quick glance at our church directory gave me the address—a small home about halfway down the street. I parked, went to the door, and rang the doorbell.

Angie answered the door. She was one of the saddest looking people I have ever seen. I introduced myself as the new pastor of the church. And she invited me in. Her home was an obstacle course of children's toys. Angie explained that she did daycare for her neighbors in her home, but the children were taking a nap and she said this was a perfect time for me to visit.

We sat down in Angie's living room, and began to talk. I told Angie about the visit in my office with her friend Ruth. Angie was very open and talked with relative ease about the daughter she never got to raise, who she and her husband named Bethany. She asked me if Ruth told me when Bethany was born. I responded that I didn't know when this had happened. Angie told me, "It was a year ago, today." I was shocked to learn that the day I visited was *the exact day*—the one year anniversary of Bethany's birth. I immediately sensed that Angie and I were a part of a divine moment. I had only a one out of 365 chance of arriving on Bethany's Birthday day. And I am not that lucky.

Angie told me the whole tragic story of Bethany's birth. She shed many sad tears as she spoke of her joy being shattered and her hope taken away. After she calmed herself she said, "We took lots of pictures. Do you want to see the pictures? Sometimes people don't want to look at them."

"I would be happy to see them," I said. We spent the next 30 minutes looking through all of the scrapbooks that contained the only photographs Angie and her husband were able to take of Bethany. They dressed Bethany in a blue denim dress with a pink collar and pink sleeves, and photographed her with each other, and with her older brothers and sisters. Consciously trying to ignore the fact that I knew the baby in the pictures was not alive, I tried to make as much fuss over the baby's beauty as I would any other baby. There were also pictures of Bethany's funeral—her casket, the flower arrangements, and the tiny little marker that rested on her grave as this world's only tribute to her very short life. Angie shed more tears as she narrated these pages of the scrapbook.

After Angie closed the final scrapbook, and put them all back on the bookshelf, she returned to her chair, and sat with her hands folded in her lap. She took a deep breath, and rested for several moments. In the silence, it was clear Angie was trying to figure out how to ask something. Finally she asked, "Pastor, there's one thing I've always wondered about. When I get to Heaven, will Bethany know that I was her mother?" The Divine moment had arrived.

There is a phrase used in the Scripture which at that moment I came to understand. *The Spirit of the Lord came upon me.* I looked directly at Angie, and waited for her to make eye contact. Then I said, "Angie, let me tell you what Heaven's going to be like. When you get to Heaven, you're going to greet all your family members: both your parents, your grandparents, and everyone else who was gone before you. They will all joyfully welcome you into Heaven, with hugs and kisses, and big smiles. Then, everyone will get real quiet. And they will all look at you and smile like they know some big secret. And then the crowd will part and move to the sides, and you will look up and see Jesus standing there, holding this little squirming baby in a blue denim dress. And he will walk up to you and place little Bethany in your arms. And he will say, "Angie, welcome to Heaven. She's been waiting for you."

I told her, "Angie, you're not just going to know Bethany in Heaven. You are going to *raise* Bethany in Heaven. I don't know if that is good theology. I don't even know if that makes sense. All I know is that Heaven is the place where everything we have lost in this world is given back to us. It's the place where God makes all things new."

Angie's tears of grief became tears of joy and hope. Momentarily, we were there; not in a different place, but in a different state, one filled with all the promise of the eternity promised to us by our God of hope.

There is a place where all the wrongs of this word are made right. We call it Heaven.

It is that place where everything taken away from us is restored.

Where relationships that have ended will start anew.

Where we are made whole again.

Where all our sad tears are turned into tears of joy, relief, and gratefulness.

That place is called Heaven. It is a real place. It is a place God made for us, to live for all eternity. It is a place of absolute perfection, wholeness and peace. It is there we rest from our labors. It is there we are reunited with loved ones. It is there we finally live in the presence of our gracious and loving Father.

It has been described as a glorious city with streets of gold, as perpetual light, as our eternal reward, as a "mansion over the hilltop," and in Kevin Kostner's movie *Field of Dreams*, as "the place where dreams come true." On the cross, Jesus described it to a thief in one word: "paradise." It is all of that, and more. It may be impossible to overstate Heaven's beauty and perfection. The apostle Paul wrote, "'What no eye has seen, what no ear has heard, and what no human mind has conceived'—the things God has prepared for those who love him . . ." (1 Corinthians 2:9 NIV).

Maybe you were encouraged not to be so "Heavenly minded" that you are "no earthly good." If you were, you were misguided. It is our right to dream, to imagine; to anticipate the place that will be our home for all eternity. The Christian life is a life lived in full expectation of Heaven. And almost all aspects of Christian discipleship point to it. Holy Communion (aka *The Lord's Supper*) is a foretaste of the Heavenly banquet we will share in God's Heavenly Kingdom. Christian fellowship is an expression of communion of all the Saints in glory. Christian action stands as an expression of our prayer for God's will to be done on earth, as it is in Heaven. The wise King Solomon was correct when he observed, "[God] has . . . set eternity in the human heart . . ." Ecclesiastes 3:11b (NIV). The more Heavenly-minded we are, the more earthly good we become!

Perhaps you were taught that Heaven is real, but that we can't know much about what Heaven is like. That's not true either. The Bible tells us a great deal about our eternal future. It describes Heaven as a place of rest, where we are reunited with our loved ones, where our aging bodies are replaced with new ones, where we celebrate the victory of love over hate, and where we see God face to face. Within the pages of this book, you will find a description of Heaven as the Scripture reveals it.

Finally, you may believe in Heaven, but you may have come to believe you can't really know if you will get in. The fact that so many people believe they can only "hope" to go to Heaven is disappointing to me—and, I believe, to God, especially when you consider everything God did to give us assurance. This is such an important issue, that I have saved it for the last chapter of the book.

I invite you to learn, to laugh, to cry, to find hope and assurance, and to realize we do not need to be afraid; in fact, we have a lot to look forward to. The more real Heaven is to you, the more your heart will yearn for that place. The guide at the back contains Bible studies you can do on your own or with a small group of friends, that will give you the opportunity to consider the ways we can experience Heaven's joys here on earth. Anticipate the future God has promised to us, and be thankful in advance for that "eternal house in Heaven, not built by human hands" (2 Corinthians 5:1b NIV).

Heavenly Rest

1

T hink about the best vacation you have ever had. My favorite vacation was the one our family took in Ontario in 1999. It was so much fun preparing for that vacation! It was also fun watching our children get ready for that vacation. Their eyes got so big when we told them we were leaving the United States and going to another country. We showed them pictures of where we were going: the CN Tower, Canada's Wonderland, and Niagara Falls. I watched with amusement as my son tried to decide which five of his Teenage Mutant Ninja Turtles figures he would take with him. It was fun to hear my daughter describe Canada as if it were the most exotic place on earth. She said to their friends, "We're going to Canada. That's in another country!" They were filled with anticipatory excitement. They counted the days up to vacation, and as the day came closer for us to go, they just couldn't sit still.

Think of your best vacation ever. It isn't just the kids who get excited. We get excited too. When we know we're going on vacation our moods are more positive, and we can handle stress more easily. Life can get so difficult, but when we know we are going on vacation, we can handle problems much better because we have something wonderful to look forward to.

The writer of the book of Hebrews says something just like that in Hebrews, chapter 11, commonly referred to as the "Faith Hall of Fame." In those verses he writes about all of the people who endured great hardship in life. He talks about Abel, Enoch, Noah, Abraham, and Sarah. He talks about how hard their lives were, especially for Abraham and Sarah, who never had a home, but who lived in tents and wandered around in the wilderness all of their lives. The writer of Hebrews says,

All these people were still living by faith when they died. They did not receive the things promised; they only saw them and welcomed them from a distance, admitting that they were foreigners and strangers on earth. People who say such things show that they are looking for a country of their own. If they had been thinking of the country they had left, they would have had opportunity to return. Instead, they were longing for a better country—a heavenly one. Therefore God is not ashamed to be called their God, for he has prepared a city for them. (Hebrews 11:13-16 NIV)

The people who followed God lived by faith; they never had the things God promised, but they could see them in the distance and knew that someday these promises would be theirs. They knew that someday they would hold them in their hands.

We have that same promise from God. Like the great old hymn says, "We're marching to Zion, beautiful, beautiful Zion. We are marching upward to Zion the beautiful city of God." This world is not our home; we are just passing through. We are headed home to Heaven, and I want you to know you are really going to love Heaven. You will just love it, and not only that, you will enjoy it!

It is not difficult to understand why the hard-laboring people of the Bible thought of Heaven as a place of rest. The earth, they believed, was a place of hardship and toil. For those people, the physical demands were oppressive. A workday dragged on from dawn to dusk. Most labor was hard, and there were only the most basic tools to make the work only slightly easier.

Though physical labor may be easier for us in the twenty-first century, emotional labor still weighs us down.

Why is life so difficult? That's a question people ask all the time. In fact there is a movie called *The Last Holiday* in which Queen Latifah plays a lady named Georgia Byrd who discovers that she has only three weeks to live. Georgia eventually learns to enjoy her last days on earth, but before she does she goes through a crisis, wondering why God has let this terrible thing happen to her. In my favorite scene, she's in church standing in her place in the choir when she spontaneously begins calling out to God, "Why, Lord? Why me?" Her outburst is an expression of her anguish, but the rest of the choir, not knowing Georgia's diagnosis, begins to join in, and pretty soon the whole church choir is singing a rousing anthem called "Why me? Why me, Lord?" The spiritual ruckus continues, and no one notices that Georgia has walked out of the church.

Now, in the movie, Georgia never gets her answer to the *why me* question. However, she does learn that she was asking the wrong question anyway. There is no answer to the why questions—not "why me?" or "why is life so hard?" Life is hard just because it is life.

But God promises that a day is coming when we can rest from our labors. There will come a time when the working tools of life will slip from our nerveless grasp. Do you know why? It is because we will not need them anymore.

Heaven is a place of rest, a place where we are not defined by the demands of life. It is a place where we are not sustained by our works. We are defined by and sustained by our relationships with God. In Heaven we don't rest because we are tired. We rest because we can.

To the biblical people, rest is not primarily about inactivity. It is an expression of our trust in the care of the God who loves us. Rest is a holy act of worship.

The Scripture describes activity and rest as a rhythm of creation. God created the world in six days, and on the seventh day he rested. He made the seventh day a holy day that came to be known as *Shabbat* (or *Sabbath*), which literally means "to stop". The Sabbath became the day when God's people honored God by resting. Resting instead of working another day was a way of acknowledging that life comes from God and not from work. The ability to work comes from God, as do work-empowering qualities like skill, creativity, determination, and motivation. We who work hard to make a living can sometimes fall into the trap of believing we are doing it ourselves. But Sabbath reminds us of the foolishness of such thinking. All that sustains life comes from God. The act of resting is therefore a proclamation of God's goodness. The old blue laws of the past captured the letter, but not the spirit of the

Sabbath principle. Rest is not merely about inactivity; it is about doing nothing other than being thankful to the true source of our lives.

Jesus once observed that his people sometimes missed the point of Sabbath by approaching it legalistically. When that occurs, rest becomes simply another type of human activity. Paradoxically, rest becomes another form of work. As a child, I remember my mother telling stories about how she raised money growing up in Rockaway Beach, New York. One of the more creative ways involved lighting ovens in the homes of orthodox Jewish families after sundown on Friday. Apparently, Sabbath custom at that time did not allow for starting a fire or any similar activity. But if a fire was already burning, it was not considered a violation of the Sabbath to use it to prepare food. So little Rosie (the Catholic girl) would knock on the doors of the apartments of orthodox Jewish families and offer to light their ovens for a nickel. After she performed her service and received her fee, meals in the Jewish household could go on as before.

When criticized for not legalistically observing the Sabbath, Jesus remarked, "The Sabbath was made for man, not man for the Sabbath" (Mark 2:27). The Sabbath was conceived as a day of Heaven on earth when we experience in small measure what we will experience for all eternity in God's heavenly kingdom. In Heaven God cares for his people, and his people celebrate their dependence on God.

It might surprise you to hear that the stress we experience in the twenty-first century has its origin in a theological heresy. We have once again eaten the forbidden fruit that gives us control over the direction of our lives. Along with that control comes the crushing stress that arises from believing that we and we alone are responsible for the quality of our lives. Immediately after we adopt that point of view, we become driven and compulsive. We find it hard to relax. Sabbath becomes impossible. The Christian gospel teaches that we are saved by the grace of God. A spiritual examination of life reveals that we are not alone, and we are only indirectly responsible for the quality of our lives. Ultimately, God is with us taking care of us. With that knowledge, we can easily relax. We can place all things into the hands of the One who feeds the sparrows and clothes the lilies. Sabbath begins.

Heaven is an eternal Sabbath on which we can finally rest. There is no stress, no work, no labor. The book of Revelation pronounces this amazing benediction upon those who live eternally in the presence of God: *"And I heard a voice from Heaven saying unto me, 'Write, Blessed are the dead which die in the Lord from henceforth:' Yea, said the Spirit, 'that they may rest from their labors; and their works do follow them'"* (Revelation 14:13).

You may have heard that verse many times at funerals or committal services. Here's how it sounds in the translation called "The Message:"

I heard a voice out of Heaven, "Write this: Blessed are those who die in the Master from now on; how blessed to die that way!"

"Yes," says the Spirit, "and blessed rest from their hard, hard work. None of what they've done is wasted; God blesses them for it all in the end" (Revelation 14:13, MSG).

Heaven is the ultimate vacation. It is our final vacation. It is the final blessing and the reward for a life lived in faith. Here on earth, there is work to be done. But in Heaven we receive an eternal vacation. Heaven is the vacation we have looked forward to all our lives. It offers us a blessed, eternal rest, which we will inherit the moment we arrive.

2

Heavenly Reunion— Explained

Will we know each other in Heaven? This is the most common concern people have about Heavenly life. Our families and friends are so important to us; so much a part of what makes life worth living, that we cannot imagine a joyful eternity without them. If Heaven turns out to be a lonely or solitary place, it simply will not be Heaven!

At an overly pious and consequently foolish time in my life, I pronounced that we shouldn't really want to see our loved ones when we get to Heaven. The only one we should want to see is God himself. If we really loved Jesus, why would we need to see anyone else, I declared.

Thankfully, reading the scripture cured me of this erroneous idea. The scripture's description of the human creation is entirely relational. From beginning of life all the way to death and beyond, the Scripture describes human beings as a family or as a community. We are a family on earth. We will be a family in Heaven.

In the book of Genesis when God created the human race he said, "let us make man in our image." Then later, when Adam was the only human being around, God said, "It is not good for the man to be alone." Note the importance of this! This is the very first time in the Scripture where something is determined to be "not good." Everything in creation was good, and the created man shared a direct intimacy with God. But that was still "not good." Human beings are created to be in relationships. Our need for other people in our lives is not a result of the fall, of weakness, or of emotional trouble. We are simply wired that way. And the reason we are that way is because the one who made us is himself that way. God said "let us make man in our image." God is one God, but God is also a relationship of Father, Son and Spirit, in which love eternally exists. Love is what it means to be God, and love is what it means to be human. We are created in the image of God as relational beings.

The second indication that we will know each other in Heaven is this: people who have died retain their earthly identity. In the Gospels' story of his Transfiguration (Matthew 17, Mark 9, and Luke 9), Jesus took Peter, James, and John to the top of a high mountain (traditionally identified as Mt. Tabor), where, amid a sublime experience, he was visited by the prophets Moses and Elijah. The Transfiguration is presented as the moment in which Heaven and earth momentarily overlap, and where Jesus is identified for the bewildered and frightened trio of disciples (and all the rest of us) as the mediator between the temporal and the eternal. What happened on that mountain was powerful and filled with many layers of meaning. But one thing is clear: Moses and Elijah, who had passed from earthly existence centuries before, maintained their individual human identity—to such an extent that the disciples who were with Jesus on the mountain easily recognized who they were.

Third: Jesus believed we would recognize each other in Heaven. This is clear from his telling of one of his more popular parables found in Luke chapter 16, the parable of the Rich Man and Lazarus. Lazarus was a beggar who pled for food at the rich man's gate. When they both died they went to the place of the departed spirits. Lazarus was in a place of comfort, and the rich man, who never showed Lazarus any kindness, was in a place of torment. The rich man saw Lazarus being comforted by Abraham, and asked Abraham to allow Lazarus to stick his finger in water and give him a drink. Abraham responded that Lazarus deserved his comfort, while the rich man, who neglected his brother, deserved no comfort at all. Jesus tells this parable, with the assumption that those who are departed can know each other and interact with the same ease they would on earth. Clearly, Jesus himself believed that people would recognize each other in the afterlife.

But perhaps the clearest statement about this was given by the apostle Paul in 2 Thessalonians chapter 4:13-18:

[13] Brothers and sisters, we do not want you to be uninformed about those who sleep in death, so that you do not grieve like the rest of mankind, who have no hope. [14] For we believe that Jesus died and rose again, and so we believe that God will bring with Jesus those who have fallen asleep in him. [15] According to the Lord's word, we tell you that we who are still alive, who are left until the coming of the Lord, will certainly not precede those who have fallen asleep. [16] For the Lord himself will come down from Heaven, with a loud command, with the voice of the archangel and with the trumpet call of God, and the dead in Christ will rise first. [17] After that, we who are still alive and are left will be caught up together with them in the clouds to meet the Lord in the air. And so we will be with the Lord forever. [18] Therefore encourage one another with these words.

The Thessalonian Christians were feeling distress over their deceased loved ones. They were wondering what happens to them—do they miss out on the kingdom of God? Paul says that, when Jesus returns, if we happen to be alive on the earth, we will meet Jesus and all those people who have gone before us in a great Heavenly reunion. We will be together with the Lord. And Paul says, that we should encourage or comfort one another with these words. What comfort would it be if we could not know each other; if we couldn't know that someone who has died is well and whole?

You see, we are made for love, and love is eternal. Even after people die, you don't stop loving them. A friend and a hospice chaplain recently described grief as "love with no place to go." But Heaven is that perfect place where love is restored, and it holds for us the promise of a blessed reunion with those who have gone before.

3

The Reunion—
Imagined

James Stuart sat contentedly in his easy chair, enjoying his favorite tea. His study was a quiet place, with rich, dark-paneled walls, and a woven carpet beneath his chair. It was early in the morning, and James was enjoying his reading of Psalm 184. James loved the quiet of the morning. There was no sound in the room except the ticking of the grandfather clock, and the soft breathing sounds of the Irish Setter curled up on the floor at his feet. James took another sip of tea, and went back to his reading. The quiet was abruptly broken by the sound of a mechanical bell. The telephone was ringing. James picked up the receiver from the hook.

"Hello?" He said. "Yes, this is Mr. Stuart . . . ." His heart began pounding as he heard the news. He was told where to go and what time to be there. He did not need to write this information down. "Yes. Thank you very much. Yes . . . I will. Goodbye." He hung the receiver on its hooks, and leaned his head back, closed his eyes, and took a deep breath. Suddenly he realized how important of a day this was going to be.

The dog's excited breathing drew him from his reverie. He opened his eyes and saw the setter, now sitting upright waiting to be informed. He reached down in patted the dog's head and rubbed his ears. "Guess what Rufus?" He said, "She's coming." The Irish setter instantly stood and barked, briskly wagging his tail. "That's right Rufus, we have to go now. She's on the *Rose of Sharon*; Dock No. 12." The young man stood up, and adjusted his sweater. He headed to the door and on the way he stopped and looked at himself in the hallway mirror. For the first time in a long time, he cared about his appearance. He looked at himself and thought, "Not bad. Except the sideburns. Much too short. Not the way she liked them at all . . . There. That's much better."

He opened the front door, and Rufus ran by, picking up his favorite ball from out of the lush grass and bringing it to his master. Stuart took the ball and threw it down the hill and watched as Rufus ran with delight to fetch it back for another round.

As he approached the road that led to the docks, James heard a bell on his left and turned and saw his friend Malcolm on his bicycle, trying to get his attention. "A beautiful morning, isn't it James?" Malcolm said.

"It certainly is Malcolm," James replied.

"Is today the day, then?"

"Yes, it is." James said, "I just received the call."

Malcolm smiled and said, "so I assume you won't be playing midfield for us this afternoon, will you?" He grinned; already knowing the answer.

"No Malcolm," James said, returning the smile, "It appears I have much more important things to do today."

Malcolm nodded and slowly pedaled away. He turned and said "Well, James. Have a wonderful day!"

"It shall be a wonderful day," Stuart thought. From the hillside looking down to the harbor, James could already see the great white ship slowly being led into the docks by the tugboats; surrounded by small sailboats, motorboats, and pleasure craft. People were already gathering at dockside, some family, some friends, and many who simply loved to welcome the new arrivals. The ship was in its final turn, slowly easing into position parallel to the dock. At full stop, its great horn sounded, joyful, loud and deep, evoking a cheer from those gathering at the harbor. Moments later, over James's left shoulder, another horn sounded, an even louder and deeper celebration. The sound came from the great temple on the mountain; the sound that everyone knew as the sound of welcome. It was one of the most joyful sounds people ever heard.

Halfway down the hill toward the docks, a young woman approached James at a rapid pace. She was skipping, dancing, almost running. She jumped on James joyfully like a cat, and hugged him excitedly. "I got the call! Did you get the call too? She's coming! That's her ship! Aren't you excited?" Rufus approached the young woman enthusiastically. She picked up the ball and threw it, giving Rufus another joyful run.

"Yes!" James said, "They just called! I don't know how I feel! It's been so long!"

The two locked arms as they continued down the hill toward the harbor. Passers-by smiled and waved and offered their congratulations and best wishes.

When they arrived at the dock, an usher, dressed in pure white, greeted them. Smiling and gesturing, he directed both of them to their place in the front, where the immediate family was invited to stand. The crowd politely parted for them, giving them the place where the ramp would be lowered to the dock. Another young couple soon joined them, and greeted them both with a hug and kiss. Everyone agreed, this was going to an amazing, wonderful day.

Finally, the ship came to a stop, its ropes were tied, and it stood motionless for several minutes. Then again, the ship's horn blasted loudly, so loudly the people covered their ears. The young man on James' left leaned over, and said, "Are you sure this is her ship, Son?"

James said, "Oh yes, she is here. I can *feel* her."

The ship then launched an enormous and amazing fireworks display. Even in broad daylight the colors were deep and rich as they burst into complex kaleidoscope shapes overhead: reds, blues and greens; bursting so loud people covered their ears again. When it ended, a respondent display began from the great temple on the mountain even more glorious and more wonderful. Lights and thunder filled the sky. From above, winged creatures descended upon the gathering crowd, filling the air with exuberant singing as they soared just over the people, dropping petals of white roses upon everyone.

The crowd cheered in celebration until a double blast of the horn of the *Rose of Sharon* announced the moment had arrived. Its engines became silent, and the people on the dock held their breath.

After two soundings of the horn from temple, a ramp slowly extended from the ship, and lowered itself to the surface of the harbor. It touched the surface of the dock only a few feet away from where James and his daughter and the family were waiting. The crowd became reverently silent. Then the young woman tightened her grip on her father's arm. "Dad . . . look! There she is!"

On the deck of the great white ship, an usher led a woman to the edge of the ramp. She held his arm tightly. She was old and moved slowly, unsteady on her feet. She wore a periwinkle dress, and a large bonnet of the same color, and a set of her favorite pearls. Her face was wrinkled and careworn, her hair gray and white, her back was crooked, and she walked slightly slumped over and with a limp. Her conductor slowly and carefully helped her down the ramp. She squeezed his arm even more tightly as she descended, and after every careful step she looked up and around, confused and bewildered, taking in the wonders of this yet unfamiliar place. She paused at the bottom of the ramp, looking at the large crowd of people gathered there. She did not yet understand why they were smiling, why they were holding each other, or why tears were falling from their eyes.

The young woman holding her father's arm leaned over and whispered into his ear, "I love this part." With some apprehension, the old woman stepped off of the ramp. As her feet touched the surface of the dock, the power of life itself rose through her from her feet through her knees, straightening her back, smoothing her skin, darkening her hair, restoring her to youthful perfection. Her body was suddenly filled with energy and strength, and she took a deep breath and spoke her first words, "Oh my goodness!" The crowd broke into amused and understanding laughter.

The conductor whispered into his charge's ear and motioned toward the man and his daughter who were anxiously waiting to welcome her. She gazed at them, causing James to quickly straighten his sweater. She took two steps toward him and looked into his eyes.

"Hello, James," she said. "You look well."

The people who heard her barely stifled their giggle. "Hello, Margaret." James said, holding back his joy, remembering everything he was taught him about how to respond to the disorientation in the newly arrived.

Margaret said, "Is this . . . am I dreaming, James? I have dreamed of you a thousand times, and when I woke up, you were not there."

James smiled and shook his head. "Not this time, dear. You're home."

Tears welled up in her eyes. Margaret dropped her purse and reached out and embraced her husband. They kissed, causing a great sigh and a cheer to erupt from the crowd. Despite the joyful lilt of the bagpipes and drums, and the celebrations from those who gathered, Jim and Margaret were alone. She whispered, "It was so lonesome without you."

He replied, "I have been waiting for you."

At the end of the embrace, Margaret turned and looked and then recognized the young lady standing next to her husband. "Violet? Yes . . . it is you isn't it?

And Margaret reached out to embrace the daughter she lost on earth many years before. "You were so young," She cried, "We tried everything. I am so sorry. The doctors didn't know what else to do."

But Violet smiled and said, "It's fine Mother. I'm fine. Look at me! I'm not sick anymore. Everything is fine."

The reunion at the harbor went on as usual, for more than several hours, as Margret greeted her parents, her grandparents, her friends, distant relatives, even Rufus, her Irish Setter. The celebration continued; a great reunion with people weeping for joy, smiling and laughing, joyful music and shouts of praise to God. Then finally it began to wane, and people slowly dispersed from the dock, to return to the activities they had planned for that day. Worship at the temple, soccer at the stadium, music at the amphitheater. There was no rush for anything. Eternity was before them all.

Reunited, James and Margret began to walk with their arms around each other up the road that led to their new home, while Violet and Rufus walked ahead, playing fetch. James asked, "How was your journey?"

Margret replied, "Not nearly what I thought it would be. James, there are so many people I want to talk to. And this place . . . well, it is so *real*!"

James smiled with understanding, "We've all been waiting for you, my Dear. But first things first—you'll spend the rest of the day with me. It's my honor to show you everything God made for us here. Then tomorrow, we'll go to the temple. We have an appointment."

She looked toward the mountain and said, "Someone up there wants to see me?"

"Yes, the one who made this place. He is more glad that you are here than the rest of us together. He spoke of you often over the past 15 years, Margaret. He is truly looking forward to seeing you."

Margaret smiled, as she looked up toward the temple, and whispered . . . *imagine that.*

James and Margaret slowly walked the path up the hill to the house. There steps were joyful, peaceful, and filled with gratitude. This was the day they both dreamed about.

Our Home on the Other Side

A woman writes, "When my three year old granddaughter Morgan came over to visit a few weeks after my husband's funeral, she looked around the room and asked, "Where's Grandpa?" I answered, "He's in Heaven."

Surprised, she looked at me and said, "Still?"

Some celebrities have unusual ideas about Heaven:

BILLY BOB THORNTON: Living on a lily pad with all the German chocolate cake and all the fried okra I could eat.

SANDRA BULLOCK: No drama—and a pint of Häagen-Dazs.

DENZEL WASHINGTON: No kids. No noise.

Jesus said, "In my father's house there are many mansions . . . ." There are people today who put the idea of owning a mansion in Heaven in the same category with people who hope for McDonald's restaurants, casinos, and resorts with free massages. The idea of having a luxurious mansion, some say, sounds so selfish and greedy. And they point out that the Greek word Jesus used means a house, a room, or a place to live. As a result, some contemporary Bible translations have dropped the word mansion. In one translation, Jesus now says, "There is plenty of room for you in my Father's home . . ." (MSG).

Whether you hope to live in a mansion or a room, you should remember how Jesus talked about Heaven. Heaven is the reverse of the world. Heaven is where the wrongs of this world are made right. Jesus taught that the first will be last and the last first. The proud will be humbled, and the humble, exalted. The greatest will be the least, and the lowly will be lifted up. And that meant something to those who followed Jesus; who came mostly from among the poor and powerless. Jesus taught that those who hardly had a place to rest on earth, would have a mansion in Heaven. That home will be for us a place of comfort and peace.

Jesus started out this talk by saying, "Do not let your heart be troubled." It's easy for our hearts to be troubled in a world like ours. Life on earth can be a whole lot of trouble. Some of that trouble is our own doing. But a lot of that trouble comes just because of the way the world is. This world is not God's home. This world does not work the way God wants it to. If it did, we wouldn't have to pray "thy kingdom come, thy will be done on earth, as it is in Heaven." So the world is a place where God's will is not always done. Sometimes it seems people are less interested in doing things God's way as time goes on. The result is, we have trouble. The lower you are on the ladder of society, the more trouble you are likely to have.

We know we live in a world of trouble. We start to get scared. But Jesus said, "Do not let your hearts be troubled, neither let them be afraid." Why not?

Because, we're headed to a place where the first shall be last and the last shall be first. We are going to where there are *many* mansions. In our world there are many poor, and only a few people get to enjoy the good life. But in Heaven—you will have the good life, and you'll have it for all eternity. That is what Jesus promised.

What this world denies us, Heaven gives us. What this world takes away, Heaven gives back. What we don't have here, we will have there, and lots of it! The Mansion is a symbol of the abundance of Heaven. We have riches in Heaven. Earth is about scarcity; about how you have to work hard every day just to pay the bills, and keep a roof over your head. But in Heaven you have a mansion—not because you earned it, but because Jesus wants to bless us with all his riches in glory.

Jesus said, "In my father's house are many mansions. I am going to prepare one for you." An earthly home is something you have to work hard to obtain and work hard to maintain. But our Heavenly home is different. Our Heavenly home is a gift—something we do not work hard to obtain or maintain. Our Heavenly home comes from Jesus. It is not the reward of a life of good works. It is a gift from our savior who loves us, in whom we put our trust.

That's why Jesus said, when he was getting ready to go, "Look, you believe in God; now believe in me . . ."

We choose to live a life of faith and trust in God. Proverbs 13:7 says, *There is one who makes himself rich, yet has nothing; And one who makes himself poor, yet has great riches.*

If we choose to live a life of faith based on trust in God, that means we may never have many of the pleasures and luxuries this world has to offer. But who cares? We have all eternity to enjoy all the riches and blessings of God. That is because of where; or really—in whom we have put our trust.

Charles Orr tells a story of a very rich man who died. One of his neighbors asked another how much the deceased had left behind. His answer was, "He left it all."

And that's the difference faith makes. Some people die leaving everything behind. But some people die with everything ahead . . . waiting for them. And the difference is, where or in whom do you trust?

That's the one thing we must be sure about. If you want eternal riches, trust Jesus. Heaven is not the reward for good people. Heaven is the gift of Jesus Christ, to the people who trust in him.

There's an old preacher's story that goes way back. I have told it myself in sermons I preached 25 years ago. And I still believe it's true, if you understand it right.

It's a story about an old man who used to build houses. He was getting old and told his boss he wanted to retire. His boss said, "Well, I understand how you feel. But I want you to do me one more favor. I want you to build me one more house. I have this great piece of property on a lake, and I would like you to build me one more house."

The builder said, "Yes" and he started building that house. But his heart wasn't in it, and so the house was not built as well as it could be. Some of the workmanship was shoddy, and some of the construction was not that good.

Finally he went to his boss and said, "OK the house is all finished." And his boss came and gave him the key to the front door. He said, "Thank you very much. This house is your house, my gift to you!"

And I have told that story to teach people that the house we will have in Heaven is a house we are building right now, through all the good things we do for God.

I still believe that as long as we remember one thing: the most important thing we can do for Jesus, is to trust him. Remember Jesus said, "Do not let your hearts be troubled. You believe in God, now believe in me." If you want a mansion, do what Jesus said: trust him! He is the builder.

Thomas asked that anxious, troubled question, "Master we don't know where you are going. How can we know the way?" Thomas was pleading for a map, a set of directions, a plan, a program, a method. He said, "Master, tell us what to do. Tell us how to get there. Show us the way."

Jesus said, "I am the way . . ." His answer intended to convey to his disciples that the way they were looking for is a person, not a map. To know the way is to know the Master. It's as if Jesus was saying, "If you want to get there, trust me. Stay with me. Depend on me. And know one thing: When I am done with your mansion, I am coming back to get you." This means the most important thing we can ever do for Jesus is to trust him. And whatever else we do for him, we do it not to get ourselves a mansion. We do it because Jesus already built us one. He has given us a home that we will enjoy for all eternity.

There was once a woman who used to clean an office building at night. She started her day in the evening, and finished in the morning. Her husband used to tell her, "You know Dear, I can pick you up in the morning when you're done work." But she would always say, "That's OK, honey, I can just take the bus." So she would take the bus home in the morning, and on that bus there were always a lot of little school children, because it was morning and they were going to school. And they would always make fun of this lady because of where she got off the bus. She would pull the cord, and the bus would stop, and the only thing around that stop was the local cemetery. The woman would get off the bus, cross the road, and go right through the main gate of the cemetery. Those little children would laugh at her and snicker, and they wondered if she was some kind of ghost. They called her the lady who lives in the cemetery.

After this happened for almost an entire school year, the bus driver thought he had to straighten those children out. So when it happened again, that the lady got off the bus and went into the cemetery, and the children were laughing at her, the bus driver looked back at them and said, "You know kids, you know that lady who you laugh at every single morning? You call her the lady who lives in the cemetery. But, you know, she doesn't really living in the cemetery. The cemetery is just a shortcut to her house." And he said to them, "she does not go *to* the cemetery, she goes *through* the cemetery, for her home is on the other side."

Jesus has given us a home on the other side. We live here in tents, because this world is not our true home. Our eternal house, not made by human hands, is waiting for us, on the other side.

5

A Heavenly Banquet

Tony and Mary were 85 years old and had been married for 60 years. Though they were far from rich, they managed to get by because they carefully watched their pennies. They were not young, but they were both in very good health, mainly because of Mary's insistence on healthy foods and exercise. One day their good health practices didn't help. They went on yet another holiday vacation and their plane crashed, sending them off to Heaven.

They reached the pearly gates, and St. Peter escorted them inside. He took them to a beautiful mansion, furnished in gold and find silks, with a fully stocked kitchen and a waterfall in the master bath. A maid was hanging their favorite clothes in the closet. They gasped in astonishment when he said "Welcome to Heaven. This will be your home now."

Tony asked Peter "How much is all this going to cost?"

St. Peter said, "Why, nothing! Remember, this is Heaven!"

Tony looked out the window and right there he saw a championship golf course, finer and more beautiful than any ever built on earth. Tony said, "How much does it cost to play out there?"

St. Peter said, "This is Heaven, You can play for free, every day."

Next they went to the clubhouse and discovered a lavish buffet lunch. Before Tony could even ask, St. Peter said "this is Heaven, it is all free for you to enjoy."

Tony looked around and said, "Where are all the low-fat and low—cholesterol and sugar-free foods?"

St. Peter said, "We don't have those. Here, you can eat and drink as much as you like and you will always be healthy. This is Heaven!"

Tony turned to his wife Mary, glared at her and said, "You and your bran flakes! We could've been here 10 years ago!"

Yes, there will be great food in Heaven. In fact, food shows up early in the Bible's description of Heaven, especially in the teaching of Jesus, where he described Heaven as a great banquet, where we all get to sit down together and feast and celebrate. In that subsistence culture in which hunger was such a common daily experience, that was a very exciting idea.

It's a little more challenging to talk about great food in our culture, where we have come to think about food almost as a health issue. We have been indoctrinated to think that any food that is delicious, sweet, savory, or rich will *kill you immediately*. It's almost like food is the enemy of our health.

While serving as a hospice chaplain, we took in a new patient named Lorraine. When Lorraine came on our service, her daughter Earlene didn't really tell her what hospice was. Lorraine knew she had cancer, but she didn't know she was dying. So, finally we talked to Earlene and explained to her the benefits her mother would experience if she knew her actual condition. Earlene was worried about how her mother would take the news, and requested that her nurse and I be present when she told her.

A few days later, we gathered in Lorraine's room, and as her mother rested in her recliner, Earlene gave her mother the news. With a low and shaky voice, she explained, "Mom, I have something to tell you. Your cancer is very bad, and, you're not going to make it."

Lorraine paused as she absorbed the news. She looked with disappointment at her daughter and said "I'm not?" Earlene quickly offered consolation, saying, "No. But mom, all these people from the hospice are here to help you. You will not be in pain, and you can do whatever you are able to do, and you can live your life from this point on any way you want to."

Lorraine thought about that, then look up hopefully. She said, "Can I eat whatever I want?"

Earlene said, "Yes, Mom, whatever you want."

Lorraine said, "Earlene, get me a bowl of chocolate ice cream, right now!" And while Earlene was in the kitchen dishing up the ice cream, Lorraine explained, "for 30 years I ate what the Doctors told me to eat. Now I am going to eat whatever I darn well please!"

And for the next 5 and half months, Lorraine feasted on all her favorite foods: Ice cream, cherry pie, Butterfingers candy bars, and Domino's pizza. She died a very happy lady, with a half-eaten piece of cheesecake on her nightstand.

Her daughter was expecting her mother to be devastated by the news, but Lorraine was liberated, because she could eat again! The fact that she was dying meant she could live it up! She didn't have to care about every morsel; or count every calorie.

Something has happened in this country related to food. It's almost like food has become the enemy. But food is not the real problem. I remember when I was a little kid, my father used to eat an enormous breakfast: 2 eggs, 2 pieces of bacon, hash browns, and a buttermilk pancake every morning. And as he was devouring that huge morning meal, Mom would put a big lunch in his lunch pail: two sandwiches, potato salad, a hard-boiled egg, a piece of fruit and some coffee. He ate like that every day of his life, and my father was skinny. But he was skinny because he worked hard all day. He moved, walked, climbed ladders, hammered nails, bent pipe and pulled wire.

I eat half as much as my father did, but I don't do nearly as much. I don't over eat, I under-move! Food is not the problem. Food is not the enemy.

In fact in the Bible, food is described as an dimension of worship. The people of Israel had a feast for every occasion. The Passover celebrated their deliverance from Egypt. The Feast of Tabernacles celebrated the wilderness years. The Feast of Trumpets consecrated each new year. The Feast of First fruits celebrated the beginning of the harvest. Pentecost was celebrated at time of the dedication of the harvest. The Feast of Purim commemorated the salvation of Israel in Persia in Esther's day.

To be a Jew in the Bible days meant to live by the theology of "God's neat; so let's eat!"

One of the best reasons to celebrate back then was a wedding. First century Jewish weddings were huge blowouts that went on for days. Jesus and his disciples attended a wedding in the town of Cana where he performed his first miracle, turning water into wine. The first miracle was not a healing or raising someone from the dead. Jesus made food. He made celebration food! Jesus ate and celebrated so much that his opponents accused him of being a drunk and a glutton. Food is not the enemy. Food is good! Wine is good!

Will there be food in Heaven? You bet your bagels there will! We will eat food not to sustain our bodies, like we do here. We will eat as an act of celebration and worship. In Heaven, you don't have to worry about cholesterol, or triglycerides or your blood sugar. You will get to eat great food, all you want and never gain a pound—I'm talking Heaven brothers and sisters!

In Revelation chapter 19, after all the doom and destruction predicted in the first 18 chapters of the book, John sees a great Heavenly gathering. He sees people from all nations, coming together to worship the almighty and victorious Jesus Christ. And the angel who conducts him through the vision tells John to write down these words: "Blessed are those who are invited to the wedding banquet of the Lamb!"

Just like Jesus promised in Matthew chapter 8, people will come from all nations and sit down together with Abraham, Isaac and Jacob, at a great Heavenly banquet, where we will celebrate the victory of Jesus over evil and darkness. It is described as a wedding feast because we will be united with him, like a bride and a bridegroom. And we will eat! We will eat great delicious food without guilt or worry; and we will eat to the honor and glory of the Lamb of God.

We will eat at that banquet to celebrate our reunion with Jesus. Jesus will eat at that banquet to celebrate his reunion with us. We are his bride. We are his beloved. When we talk about Heaven, we often talk about what a joy it will be to see Jesus face to face. But have you ever thought that it's going to be just as joyful for Jesus to see us face to face?

In Matthew 26, Matthew remembers how they all sat down with Jesus on the night before his death, and ate the Passover. And he remembers that . . .

[26] *While they were eating, Jesus took bread, and when he had given thanks, he broke it and gave it to his disciples, saying, "Take and eat; this is my body."*

[27] *Then he took a cup, and when he had given thanks, he gave it to them, saying,* "Drink from it, all of you. [28] This is my blood of the covenant, which is poured out for the forgiveness of sins.

The other Gospels record it pretty much the same way. But Matthew remembers one other thing Jesus said; something that must have hit him hard and stayed with him. In verse 29, Jesus said: *I tell you, I will not drink from this fruit of the vine from now on until that day when I drink it new with you in my Father's kingdom.*

The Bible says only a few things about the heavenly existence of Jesus. He certainly spends a great deal of time praying for us. I'm sure he does a lot of other things. But one thing he does not do: He does not eat or drink—not as an act of celebration. Jesus cannot celebrate in Heaven until we get there. That's how much you and I mean to him. It will only be Heaven for Jesus when you and I are there.

When Christians gather to celebrate Holy Communion, it is in anticipation of that banquet we will enjoy in Heaven. It is small and is made of only bread and wine. But like a good appetizer, it is intended to make us want more.

When we receive this meal, we remember how he died for us, but we also remember what he promised—that a great banquet is waiting for us; a banquet he is preparing.

Oh, you are really going to love Heaven! Because when we all get there, we will all sit down together and eat. And from that day on, we will enjoy the bounty of his goodness for all eternity.

6

A New You

For all the young people reading this book, let me share with you a very important piece of wisdom, which I learned the hard way: *never have a child after you're 40.* I know the trend is for young couples to wait to have their children. But there is one big drawback of having a child at age 40 or later: that child will quickly be able to outrun you. Having a toddler who is faster than you makes parenting much more difficult. When my older children were new to the bipedal world, they were easy to catch. If they picked up a pair of scissors or some other sharp object they were not supposed to have, I would confront them and demand, "Give me that!" Only once did each of them scan the room, looking for an escape route. When they took that first step in the wrong direction, I quickly pounced on them, and instantly removed the dangerous object from their hand. Though they were little children, they learned quickly. They never tried to run again.

Not so with my youngest child, born when I was 40 years old. If she had something she was not supposed to have, and I demanded it, she would *always* run. She knew that I could not catch her as easily. When she turned three, she developed a contemptuous way of looking at me when I demanded she give me something she shouldn't have. I called it the, "Yeah, right, old man" look.

My youngest daughter could come out of her room carrying a loaded bazooka, and all I could say was, "Honey, remember to put that away when you're done playing with it." I was 40. My body was already beginning to show its age. My daughter is 18 now. Not only can she outrun me. She can out-everything me. Sad.

Do you remember when you had lots of energy? Oh how the body groans as we age! As I am typing this manuscript I find myself having to take frequent breaks because my 57 year old hands hurt. When this first started I would rub my hands together and think—what did I do yesterday to make my hands hurt? Did I bang my hand in a door, or carry something heavy or use them in some unusual way? But now I know—it's my old uncle Arthur (itis) coming to visit!

The biblical way of talking about this is to say that our bodies are perishable, or subject to decay. That sounds kind of extreme. It makes it sound like zombies from the movie *Night of the Living Dead*. But it actually means something we all know to be true—that our bodies do not stay in their pristine and optimal condition. We age. We decline. We hit our peak in our teens, 20's or sometime 30's, and then suddenly we are over the hill.

In the UK they call senior citizens "coffin dodgers." Isn't that awful? But as we age, we feel as if we are playing hide and seek with the grim reaper. The body, which was once young and filled with vitality, begins to groan with the sufferings and struggles of aging.

The Biblical explanation for that, found the book of Genesis, is that after Adam and Eve ate from the fruit of the tree of the knowledge of good and evil, they were alienated from God, from each other, and even from themselves. But they had not yet eaten from the tree of life. God removed them from the garden, an act which is sometimes seen as cruel banishment, but was really for their protection. If they had eaten from the tree of life after the fall, they would have become immortal, their sinful state would have become permanent, and humanity would have been lost. But God allowed death so he would have a way to redeem us. How? By coming to this world incarnated in the man Jesus, and do the one thing he had to become a man to do: die for our sins.

So when we are young, we see death as a curse that takes our loved ones away, and will one day claim us too. But death (the death of Jesus) is how God has saved us, and through death we arrive at the fullness of our redemption.

A little boy asked his mother what death was like. She said, "It's like the time you fell asleep in the living room. Your dad picked you up and carried you to your bedroom, and the next morning when you woke up you were there. So when you die, it's like falling asleep in one place, and our Heavenly father picks you up, and when you wake up, you're in a different place." I love that explanation, except that what the apostle Paul would add to that is that not only are you in a different place, YOU are different!

You get a new body in Heaven, one that is not perishable, not subject to decline! Your new body does not age, does not hurt, and you never die. In Heaven, you can eat of the tree of life, and you live forever.

When we go to Heaven, we are not transparent entities that you can stick your hand through. We have real bodies similar to the ones we have now, except that it is not subject to the ravages of time. In Philippians 3:201-21 (NIV), Paul says: *We eagerly await a Savior . . . the Lord Jesus Christ, who, by the power that enables him to bring everything under his control, will transform our lowly bodies so that they will be like his glorious body.*

So when we get to Heaven, we will be transformed and given a body that is like Jesus' resurrection body. Jesus lived on earth in his resurrection body for 40 days, then he ascended into Heaven. He was not a ghost; he was *him*. This is what theologians call *continuity*. Our earthly and Heavenly bodies are different, but our identity is maintained. You have a new body, but you are still *you*. The first people who saw Jesus raised from the dead had a little trouble recognizing him, which might have been because nothing like a resurrection had ever happened before. But eventually they realized it truly was Jesus. He may have looked slightly different, maybe a little younger . . . who knows? But it was him! This is continuity—the old body is transformed into the new, but the self is retained.

Second, our new body will be set to a state of optimal health and wholeness. In 2 Corinthians, Paul describes our earthly body as a tent, and our heavenly body as a house. A tent is a temporary home, used for a specific purpose. It is a workable shelter, but does not have the amenities of a house. I can live in a tent for about a week. But then I want to go back to my house, where it's warm, and dry, and a hot shower awaits me! You will not believe the energy you are going to have in Heaven! If you have not walked in a long time, you are going to run like the wind! If you have a hard time remembering things, in Heaven you will have a clarity of mind that will shock you. And if you have lost a part of your body because of surgery, you will get that part back in Heaven.

A young mother was struggling with the impending death of her son, who was sick with leukemia. Every night she would pray for her son to get well, but his disease only advanced. One night was particularly dark, when her son was sick from chemotherapy. She sat on the bed and prayed, demanding that God made her son well. She became angry as she pointed out the injustice of evil people living to old age while her wonderful son faced death. The boy, passing by his mother's room, heard her angry conversation through the slightly open door. He entered the room and said reassuringly, "Mom, don't be mad at God. He told me that when I get to Heaven, I can have my hair back. He's right—you get everything back. Your Heavenly body will be perfectly whole.

Third—our new bodies will be the perfect vehicles through which we can love God and love each other. Think for a minute about Jesus' body. When he was raised from the dead, he showed himself to his disciples, and one of them, Thomas, was not there. So when he rejoined the group, they said, "Thomas, Jesus is alive!" But he didn't believe him. He thought they were pulling a prank.

Then shortly after, Jesus appeared again. He held out his hands and said, "Thomas, here. Put your fingers in the holes in my hands and feet, and put your hand in my side, and see that I am really here."

Why did Jesus still have the marks of crucifixion even in his resurrection body? It was because they are the marks of love. Those marks are not scars. They are there to remind us, for all eternity, of how much Jesus loved us, and how all we enjoy in Heaven is because he died our death on earth.

Our heavenly bodies will be the perfect vehicle for us to express our love: we'll have hands to hold, arms to hug, and vocal chords to use to sing in praise. One of our problems here on earth is we use our bodies for all the wrong things: for violence, for hurting, or for war. We only will have to love in Heaven, and our new bodies will be perfect for it; which means we really have a lot to look forward to.

Pastor Rande Smith describes it as like the joy you feel when you buy a new car. Use your imagination. Let's say you've decided to go to a dealership here in the area and buy the car of your dreams. Maybe it would be a luxury SUV like an Escalade, or a sports car like a Ferrari, or a great truck like the Nissan Titan. Whatever your dream vehicle is, that's what you are going to buy. So you buy it, and are told it will be ready for you tomorrow. So they've already taken your old car as a trade-in, which means that you have no way to get to the dealership tomorrow . . . so you'll need to get a taxi to take you on the 10 minute ride over there.

Now, when you're riding over to the dealer in this cab, how much time would you spend thinking about the taxi itself? You don't notice its paint job, or the size of its engine, or the quality of its stereo system. You don't try to fix the torn upholstery in the taxi cab. Why not? Because you're only going to be in the car for 10 minutes, and you've got the car of your dreams waiting for you where you are going!

You're thinking about that car! You are imagining yourself behind the wheel of that amazing ride, and you couldn't care less if the taxi has a dent, or a broken headlight.

The Scripture says that our life on this planet is the 10-minute cab ride to eternity. Hosea 13:3 says our lives are "like the morning mist, like the dew that vanishes early in the day." And yet we get so preoccupied with that earthly "cab" that we're running around in that we forget the car we have waiting for us!

We spend all kinds of time and energy and money on health clubs, diets, stylish clothes. We take these bodies to doctors and dentists and optometrists and even cosmetic surgeons. We spend money on haircuts and manicurists . . . all this on these bodies that are here today and gone tomorrow.

It is right to care for our earthly bodies as well as we are able. But we should spend a lot more time looking forward to, and being thankful for, the body we will have in Heaven, which the scripture promises us will be "as glorious as Jesus' own glorious body."

If that dream car waiting for you at the lot, was not something you bought for yourself, but something your best friend gave you, at great sacrifice to himself, you might think about spending that cab ride writing a thank you note, or thinking of ways you can show how grateful you are that you don't have to drive around in that old clunker anymore.

Oh, you are really going to love Heaven! And you are really going to love the new body you have in Heaven. A glorious body, just like one Jesus has, transformed by the one who makes all things new.

7

The Place Where All is Well

My teenage daughter is a healthy eater. When other teens reach for potato chips, she opens her bag of carrots. She came home late one evening, and announced that she was going to the kitchen to make a salad. Soon, I could hear, just above the sound of the televised basketball game, the rhythmic sound of chopping carrots. The chopping went on for several minutes, until it was interrupted by a piercing scream. I immediately leaped up and ran toward to the kitchen, trying to remember what I was taught in basic first aid about stopping profuse bleeding or preserving a detached finger. I ran into my terrified daughter at the kitchen door.

"Are you alright?" I shouted. She did not answer until after she had climbed the sofa. She picked up a pillow, clutching it to her body like a shield. "Dad!" she cried, "There's a mouse in the kitchen!" She screamed the word *mouse* as if it were a synonym for *Tyrannosaurus*.

Amused, I did the worst thing a parent could do. I gave her a rational explanation of why she did not need to be afraid. I pointed out the size differential between the mouse and her. I offered her the hollow proverb, "that mouse was more scared of you than you were of it," which, of course, was no comfort at all, and only resulted in her becoming both terrified and annoyed.

I was immediately ordered by my terrified daughter to rid the world of this invasive creature. I agreed to this task only because it was clear that no one was going to sleep that night if the rodent were left to roam. So I put a standard mouse trap on the kitchen floor, along the baseboard where she spied the creature, and within the hour we heard a telltale *snap*: the familiar sound of a mouse meeting its maker! One plastic bag and a trip to the garbage can later, the mouse was gone. Peace was restored.

Biologists have their own explanation of why we human beings are afraid of such little things. It goes back to the time when we lived in trees and in caves, when the primary threats to our existence were not the large predators, but the tiny things that creep and crawl, that sting, inject venom, and carry disease.

The Biblical account of creation speaks to a larger question: *What has gone wrong with the world?* If the world was created by God, who, at every stage declared it good, why has our world become such a broken place? The reason, in a word, is sin.

Sin is the reason creation fears us and we fear it. Sin is the reason we fear each other. Sin is the reason we fight wars. Sin is the reason there are prisons. Sin is the reason we find it so hard to have close, happy relationships. Sin is the reason there are hate crimes. Sin is the reason we have to be afraid to go out at night. Sin is the reason we can't be the people we want to be.

Sin has completely disfigured this world and everyone in it. It is the disease no one talks about. I have it, and so do all of you. Even those of us who by the grace of God have found the cure still get an attack of it every once in a while.

Being sick with this disease was one of my earliest memories. When I turned 5 years old, Mom and Dad gave me a new red tricycle for my birthday. The day I received it, no one could get me off of it. I sat on it all morning, and pedaled it in a tight circle around the living room.

At noon I was still sitting on the tricycle watching Bozo's Circus on TV. After Bozo lead the grand march and his show was over, the news came on. I listened to the man on the news tell a story about a mother who drowned her baby in the bathtub. I remember being very upset by that story. I enraged at that mother, so much so that I acted out. I turned my tricycle around and started running it over and over again into my mother's new white sofa, pretending it was that evil Mother. When Mom saw what I was doing, she yanked me off the tricycle and put me in my room, and I didn't get to ride my tricycle for a month. All she saw were the black marks on the sofa. She didn't even care about the mother who drowned her baby in the bathtub.

I think maybe that it was about that time in my life that I started to feel the effects of this disease. Martin Luther called it "curvature of the soul" because of the way it distorts our spiritual lives. King David described it as a heavy weight we carry around without knowing it. He said in Psalm 38:4, *My guilt has overwhelmed me like a burden too heavy to bear.* Sin crushes us, and disables us. We live in a world that is sick because we have stopped trusting in God.

Jesus came into the world to heal us from this disease. We can see that healing was his priority by taking note of the people Jesus reached out to. Shortly after calling the notorious tax-collector Matthew to be his disciple, Jesus had the following confrontation with the Pharisees, found in Matthew chapter 9:

⁹ As Jesus went on from there, he saw a man named Matthew sitting at the tax collector's booth. "Follow me," he told him, and Matthew got up and followed him.

¹⁰ While Jesus was having dinner at Matthew's house, many tax collectors and sinners came and ate with him and his disciples. ¹¹ When the Pharisees saw this, they asked his disciples, "Why does your teacher eat with tax collectors and sinners?"

¹² On hearing this, Jesus said, "It is not the healthy who need a doctor, but the sick. ¹³ But go and learn what this means: 'I desire mercy, not sacrifice.'[a] For I have not come to call the righteous, but sinners."

Jesus' words should not be misunderstood. The Pharisees, known for their piety, were not truly righteous. They had the same disease, but they always denied it, so there wasn't any way for Jesus to help them. Instead, he reached out to the people who were most disfigured by sin: like people who were trying to make quick money by colluding with the Roman government. Jesus reached out to people like Matthew and his friends. When the Pharisees criticized Jesus for his interest in such people, he said, "Look, only the sick people need a doctor. People like you, who think they are whole, think you need no help."

Everywhere Jesus went, he healed people from the disease of sin. He changed people's lives, and when he was nailed to the cross, this disease we carry was nailed there too. Because of what Jesus did, we are being healed from this disease. But we're not totally free from it yet. Paul spoke about that in the Book of Romans chapter 7:

[15] *I do not understand what I do. For what I want to do I do not do, but what I hate I do.* [16] *And if I do what I do not want to do, I agree that the law is good.* [17] *As it is, it is no longer I myself who do it, but it is sin living in me.* [18] *For I know that good itself does not dwell in me, that is, in my sinful nature.* [c] *For I have the desire to do what is good, but I cannot carry it out.* [19] *For I do not do the good I want to do, but the evil I do not want to do—this I keep on doing.* [20] *Now if I do what I do not want to do, it is no longer I who do it, but it is sin living in me that does it.*

[21] *So I find this law at work: Although I want to do good, evil is right there with me.* [22] *For in my inner being I delight in God's law;* [23] *but I see another law at work in me, waging war against the law of my mind and making me a prisoner of the law of sin at work within me.*

Paul candidly and honestly describes human nature when he said, "I want to do what is good and right. I don't want to do evil." But then "what happens is I end up not doing what I want to do. I do the very thing I don't want to do." Does that sound familiar? No one wakes up in the morning and says, "Today I am going to be selfish and insensitive and I'm going to kick the dog!" Yet, honesty demands that we admit there are days when that's exactly what we do. We end up hurting ourselves and the people we love. Paul explains this clearly: "If I want to do good and instead do evil, it is not me who is doing it. It is the sin that still lives in me." It's the disease that still asserts itself and disables us.

Dwight L Moody used to tell about elephants. Dwight L Moody visited a circus that came to Chicago one summer. The circus owner gave Moody a private tour. At one point they came upon the place where the elephants were kept. Moody noticed something odd. The young elephants were held to a stake by a heavy chain around one leg, while the mature elephants were held by just a small rope. Moody thought it should be the other way around.

But when he asked about it, the circus owner explained that when the elephants are young, they pull against the chain, but eventually they learn the chain can't be broken, and they give up. So when the elephant gets old, they only have to use a rope, because when the elephants pull and feel the resistance, they assume they can't break it. They just stop trying.

Moody said, "My friend, I know many believers in the same predicament. Christ has freed them from sin, but they keep living in sin, because they just don't know how free they are."

That is why we have those regretful moments Paul talked about. Christ has freed us from our disease, but we still feel the effects of it once in a while. Because we know the price that was paid to free us from this disease, the way it continues to show up in our lives is heartbreaking to us.

That is another reason Heaven is a place we can look forward to! Heaven is the place where we can finally be free. It is the place where we are healed from this curvature of the soul and all its effects.

In Heaven we will have no desire to sin anymore. We will want only to love God and love each other.

In Heaven we will not have the temptation to sin anymore. We live in a world now that constantly tempts us every single day. But in Heaven those temptations will be gone.

In Heaven, we will be entirely whole; free from this disease, 100 percent healed and free from the burden of sin. We've been carrying this burden around so long we don't even know what it's like to live without it. But in Heaven we will know. We will finally be free.

We will be free because we will live in the presence of the One whose love heals us completely. And it is in his presence that we will finally be the people he created us to be. The cure begins when we trust in Jesus. And the cure is complete when we see him face to face.

Back in 1988 I got a call from a woman I didn't know. She seemed kind of nervous on the phone; and she was acting a little reluctant to tell me what she was calling about. Finally she said, "I was wondering if you could visit my brother in the hospital."

I said, "Sure I'd be happy to."

She said, "Well before you say yes, there's something you should know—my brother is dying of aids." And she said, "We used to go to church when we were little, and I know he needs the Lord now. You're the fifth pastor I've called. No one would see him, and the last one I talked to said my brother's disease was God's punishment for his sin, and he would not go either."

I said, "I'll go see your brother." But after I hung up the phone, I started to pray, "Father, what do you want to say to this young man?"

Within a few minutes I was at the reception desk of Memorial Hospital, and I asked about this young man. They gave me a room number on the fifth floor. So I got on the elevator, with a mother and her little boy, and a nurse carrying a clipboard. And as we all rode the elevator up, the nurse said, "He sure is being brave about all this." But when I looked at the boy, he seemed anything but brave. He looked scared to death. His eyes were big, his arms were tight and he was pulling on the fingers of one hand with the other. I don't know what was happening to that little guy. Maybe he was just getting his tonsils out. Or maybe he was having some tests or a even maybe a serious procedure. I didn't know. But I kept looking at his eyes, and my heart went out to him because of how frightened he looked. And when he and his mom and the nurse got off at the 4th floor, after the elevator door closed, I prayed, "Father, whatever that little guy is going through, please be with him. Make it easy for him."

I got off at my floor, and found the room were Jeremy was. I walked into his room, and before I could introduce myself, I noticed something. This was a young man in his mid-20's, but his eyes were the same as that little boy's eyes in the elevator. He looked just as scared, and just as unsure as the frightened little child. And immediately my heart went out to him. I saw him, not as a man with a disease many people blamed him for, but as a young man with the same problem as all the rest of us. I decided that he needed the same thing we all need. He needed the grace of God. He needed the love of Jesus.

So when I talked to him he told me he was a Christian, but he wondered how God could ever accept him. He felt he never had much of a chance to do anything to show God he cared about him.

I reminded him about what Jesus said to the thief on the cross, a most moving moment in the passion story from Luke chapter 23:

[39] *One of the criminals who hung there hurled insults at him: "Aren't you the Messiah? Save yourself and us!"*

[40] But the other criminal rebuked him. "Don't you fear God," he said, "since you are under the same sentence? [41] We are punished justly, for we are getting what our deeds deserve. But this man has done nothing wrong."

[42] Then he said, "Jesus, remember me when you come into your kingdom."

[43] Jesus answered him, "Truly I tell you, today you will be with me in paradise."

The thief trusted Jesus in his dying moment. He never went to church, never took communion, never sang a hymn, never gave an offering. He never even had a chance to go back and make amends for what he had done.

But Jesus made this promise to that man: *"Today, you will be with me in paradise."*

It amazes me that people today still wonder: am I good enough to get into Heaven? Have I done enough? We don't understand that trying to be good enough is a part of the disease. Trusting in Jesus is the cure. Heaven is the place where we will be finally, totally and eternally healed from the disease that not only makes us sick, but makes us blind to how sick we are. Oh, you're really going to love Heaven, because when you get to Heaven, you will find for the first time, that you are utterly, and totally free.

Heavenly Worship

8

I was a new pastor of a new church in a new town. I got a call my first day in the office from a colleague who graciously invited me to attend the upcoming meeting of the local ministerial association. I thought of this as a great opportunity to meet my brothers and sisters of the clergy, so I went. I was greeted enthusiastically by the reverends of the different denominations represented in our small town. They welcomed the new preacher in town with warmth and excitement. There was no hint of arrogance or competition. The Roman Catholic auxiliary bishop hugged me (he was dressed in blue jeans and a sweater). The African Methodist Episcopal pastor called me his brother. They made me feel that I was home! It was almost overwhelming! I felt immediately I had come to a special place. I just knew I would find this new collegiality refreshing.

As the reverends were finishing the Amish cake provided by the host church, someone asked the group if anyone had heard about what was happening at a church that was not represented at that meeting; a church called Calvary Temple. Calvary, a self-described non-denominational church just outside of town, was experiencing a boom! Its parking lot was always full. Its worship center jam-packed with people (while many of our churches were at least half-empty). Finally one pastor remarked, somewhat contemptuously, "That Church puts on such a show on Sunday morning. And there are always people who want Church to be nothing but a good show." On the other side of the table, another pastor responded "What's wrong with putting on a show, as long as it's a really great show?"

The collegiality ended.

Our ministerial gathering quickly became polarized around how much "show" a worship service should be. The pastors who complained about Calvary's "show" were quickly rebuked by their brethren who pointed out that a pipe organ is a much more formidable instrument than an electric guitar. Stained-glass windows can be seen as equally showy as spot lights. The preacher in blue jeans is no less admired as the preacher in liturgical robes (though one pointed out that Calvary's preacher should be admired for being able to look presentable in jeans, whereas many of us at the table were not so gifted in the waistline). In the end, the gathering came to an uneasy truce. We admitted that worship, whether contemporary or traditional is a kind of show. However it fails to be worship if we forget who the show is for. To qualify as worship the show must be for God.

Worship is a show; a display—of our love and our gratitude to God. God enjoys our songs, our praise, and our prayers. If our show of love didn't matter to God, we would never need to worship. We could all sleep in, and our Church buildings could be divided into apartments or offices.

The Danish Philosopher Kierkegaard was trained to be a pastor. But he soon left the church because he was dissatisfied with many things, especially with worship. He critically said that worship services were like theater productions: The pastor was the performer, God was the prompter, and the people were the audience. But he said if the church really were a theater, the pastor would be the prompter, the people would be the performers, because *God is the audience.* The show is not for you and me. Christian worship is a performance of praise to God.

It isn't forbidden that worship should affect us. You come to church sad and disheartened and you leave encouraged. You walk in tired, plop down in the pew, and by the end of the service you are energized. You come in worried, and you leave reassured by the presence of God. That's all a part of worship too! But worship has that effect because it gives us an opportunity to forget about ourselves and our problems, and to set our hearts on the One who is greater than our problems. We talk a lot in church these days about the style or worship. Style is less important than the heart of worship, which is to meet the one who is eternally good and gracious and loving, and who is taking care of us down to the minutest detail, and will continue watching over us until the day we go home to his heavenly kingdom, where we worship not because we need to, but because we love to.

That brings to the book of Revelation, and its unveiling of a Heavenly show of worship in Revelation chapter 5. John writes:

Then I looked, and I heard around the throne and the living creatures and the elders the voice of many angels, numbering myriads of myriads and thousands of thousands, saying with a loud voice, "Worthy is the Lamb who was slain, to receive power and wealth and wisdom and might and honor and glory and blessing!" And I heard every creature in Heaven and on earth and under the earth and in the sea, and all therein, saying, "To him who sits upon the throne and to the Lamb be blessing and honor and glory and might for ever and ever!" And the four living creatures said, "Amen!" and the elders fell down and worshiped. (Revelation 5:11-14, NIV)

God gave that vision to John to speak to the needs discouraged Christians all over the world. At that time many were being persecuted by the Emperor of Rome. Others were struggling; attempting to evangelize while being ignored by their pagan neighbors. To these people and to us, who struggle daily with the troubles and challenges of life, God presents a show; a great drama of worship: with wonderful music, angelic choirs, flashes of light and peals of thunder. But at the center of this display is a lamb; a lamb that has the wounds of ritual sacrifice, but who is still alive. This is the Lamb of God, Jesus Christ, the savior of the world, who is worshipped along with God, who sits on the throne. The greatest, deepest, and most intense worship is for Jesus, the one who represents everything God has done for us.

That's why worship makes a difference! We are worshiping the One who has given us the greatest gift ever given. Pagans worship in the hope of gaining God's favor. But we worship because God has already given us his favor. The Lamb has been slain. Salvation has come. His goodness and his love is the reason we worship.

A few years ago I went to my office and found a letter on my desk from someone I didn't know. The letter said. "We are from Deerfield and were in town last weekend because our son who goes to college in Grand Rapids was in an automobile accident, and is in the hospital, still in a coma. Thank you for the beautiful worship service."

I was a little embarrassed because before I could write back, I had to struggle to remember what I had preached about that Sunday. I am certain that it was not anything I said that helped this family. It's that they had the opportunity to have an encounter with our compassionate and comforting God, who is always near. But we approach God with heightened sensitivity when we gather with God's people for worship. We come to church with problems, and we meet the God who is greater than our problems, bigger than our pain, and more able to forgive than we are able to fail. We find him in music that inspires, in preaching that challenges, and in the people who offer their love and support. God is on the throne, as John described. But God is also inhabits the people who praise him.

Here on earth we worship because we need the power of God's presence to cope with how hard life can be. But in Heaven we are finally and eternally whole, free from sorrow, worry and pain. In that heavenly context our worship will be our sincere expression of gratitude. We will join with all creation in earth and in Heaven to thank God for his love, and his salvation.

Worship in Heaven is awesome and tremendous and beautiful. The sounds and sights and even the smells of heavenly worship will blow you away. But the most crucial thing about Heavenly worship is not how it happens, but why. The moment when the Lamb of God appears we all will be struck by the revelation that his love, not our goodness, is what gave us our place in his heavenly congregation. Our worship is our response to grace.

I have a colleague named Dan who illustrates the meaning of grace this way: Dan describes himself as a country boy, who one day met Jane, who was from a wealthy family. Dan fell in love with Jane first, before Jane fell in love with him. So when Dan realized how he felt about Jane, he went on a program to transform himself into the kind of man he thought Jane could fall in love with. He started doing all kinds of strange uncharacteristic things to make himself worthy of Jane's affections. He started taking two showers every day, because he never wanted to smell like the barn (nor what is inside the barn) when he was around Jane. He changed the way he dressed. He changed the way he wore his hair. And if he was taking Jane out for dinner, he would always find the restaurant first, and then he would go pick Jane up. He never wanted to get lost when they were together. He wanted her to feel that he was always in control, so that she would be so impressed that she would fall in love with him. And apparently, it worked; because when Dan asked her to marry him she said, "Yes."

So Dan and Jane were married shortly after they both graduated from college. Dan followed a call into ordained ministry, and enrolled in seminary and he and his new bride settled into a little apartment nearby Dan's seminary campus.

Dan recalls that that's when he started to realize what a predicament he had gotten himself into. Dan found himself married to a beautiful and bright woman, and he was not sure if the man she was in love with was the real Dan. In the context of 24/7 life together, Dan found he could not hide his real personality. Dan began to feel very insecure.

Of course, Jane was never fooled by Dan's attempt to hide his true self. She came up with her own way to reassure him; a phrase that she used many times throughout their forty years of marriage. Whenever Dan would do something "manly," like get them totally lost while pretending to know exactly where they were, Jane would look at Dan with a smile and would say, "Daniel, it's a good thing you didn't do this before I agreed to marry you." Her reassurance did not even need to be spoken. "But now that I am your wife, I'm sticking with you no matter what!"

Dan says, "I thought I had to change myself to get someone to love me. But the truth is, that I could never really change until I met the one who loved me whether I changed or not."

And that's also true of our relationship with God. We don't worship to get God to love us. We worship because God is great enough to love us even when we couldn't care less about him. God sent his son, Jesus Christ the Lamb of God, into the world when the world was still in darkness. We broke his body. We shed his blood. He still bears on his heavenly body the marks of what we, the human race, did to him. Yet, according to God's plan, the moment of Christ's great sacrifice became the moment of redemption and transformation for all mankind . . . for you, and for me.

This is the one gracious act that gives us our best reason to worship. If God never did another thing for us, that one act or benevolent mercy would be enough to inspire and eternity of worship.

The End of Tears

9

Thirty years of ministry have brought me the privilege to perform the funeral service for many congregants and many dear friends. I have been with many families in their home or in the hospital room, and have witnessed that holy moment when a family says good-bye to someone they love as they leave this world. I have been witness to grief many times, and have offered comfort in times of human loss on countless occasions.

But I have never witnessed grief so profound or deep as the grief I encountered almost 20 years ago in the emergency veterinary hospital. We had just adopted our first pet, a kitten we named Molly, who had just been spayed. On Thanksgiving night after our holiday meal, the place on Molly's tummy where the vet glued the incision together seemed to be coming apart. It did not look right. So I drove Molly down to the veterinary emergency room in Grand Rapids, the only place in a 100 mile radius that was open on Thanksgiving for pet emergencies. The doctor examined Molly and explained that what was happening was serious but easily treatable. He recommended a simple procedure and a night in hospital for observation. He promised me she would be fine the next morning. Ironically, when the veterinarian told me how much that procedure was going to cost, I did indeed grieve deeply, and shed a few tears, but for a totally different reason.

While I was waiting in the lobby, a family came in carrying their chocolate brown lab, which was clearly very sick. There were at least

10 people in that family; Mom and Dad, a couple grandparents, and at least six children of various ages. The vet put Molly in a cage so he could deal with the immediate situation. From the lobby I could easily hear what was happening in the examination room. The moment the family laid their beloved Rex on the examination table, the dog expired. The weeping and wailing I heard on the other side of the door was both loud and deep. I had never heard such an outpouring of grief, not even in a hospital room or the Emergency Room! The family emerged from the room crying and holding each other. They were consoling the little ones and passing around a box of tissues. They left the hospital still pouring out their sadness.

At first I was somewhat annoyed by this seemingly overly dramatic display. But since that time our cat Molly lived out her life and passed away, and a year later our sheltie, sick with cancer, also had to be put down. In addition I have experienced the loss of both parents, a few close friends, and many brothers and sisters of the local churches I have served. I now understand that whether we are mourning for a pet or a person, we mourn for the same reason. Their passing creates in our lives a series of *no mores*. The *no mores* are the things that come to an end. No more walks in the park. No more curling up on my lap. No more warm body next to me at night. The *no mores* are the reason we mourn. The *no mores* are the reason the tears come. Life has a way of handing up one *no more* after another. Some of those losses are not the loss of a person, but the loss of an ability. No more driving. No more walking. Whenever anything comes to an end, the *no more experience* visits us. And with the *no mores* come the most profound grief of life.

But that's why you're really going to love Heaven! Because in Heaven, there are no more *no mores*. The Bible says God will wipe away the tears from our eyes, *"There will be no more death, or mourning or crying or pain, for the old order of things has passed away"* (Revelation 21:4). In Heaven, there are no more *no mores*. No more reason to mourn. No more good byes. No more funerals. No more wheelchairs. No more sickness! I don't know what Doctors are going to do in Heaven.

I once teased a surgeon who attended a Bible Study I led about not having anything to do in Heaven. He said, "I know what I'm going to do in Heaven. I'm going to play the guitar." And he told us that when he became a surgeon, his mentors made him give up playing the guitar, because playing the guitar causes calluses to form on the tips of your fingers, and you can't have calluses if you are going to be a surgeon. So even becoming a doctor created a *no more* for him—no more guitar playing! The good doctor said whimsically, "I don't want to play a harp in Heaven. I want to play a 1969 Les Paul Custom sunburst with gold-plated pickups." Rock on, Doc.!

There are no more *no mores* in Heaven. There are no endings. There are no losses. And even the losses that we have suffered here on earth are made right. Every tear we have shed is dried in Heaven—by God himself.

God is the one who makes all things new—so no matter what you have seen on earth, God has something greater in store for us in Heaven. And that is why there are no more tears. All the ugliness of life is gone, and even the beauty of earthly life is replaced by sights and sounds we cannot even imagine. We've lived here so long, and shed so many tears, that we can't even imagine the world God has waiting for us. We come to God like Mary and Martha came to Jesus when their brother Lazarus died (John 11). They were glad that Jesus came, but in their grief they did not really understand the possibilities. Jesus wept, because Lazarus was dead, but then he raised him from the dead, because he is the Son of God. Our vision of what Heaven is like is often only a slight improvement of the earth. But God did not promise just to improve things. He promised to make all things new.

There will always be tears on earth. As long as there are *no mores*, we will shed the tears that come with them. But in Heaven, there are no more *no mores*. And that is why I am supremely confident that you are really going to love Heaven! You really are! You'll love it because there is no more sorrow. No more crying. No more pain. No more curse. No more suffering. No more hunger. No more thirst. No more night. And no more death.

We will never again have reason to cry, unless it is for the joy of worship, or of blessed reunion with Christ and our loved ones. There are no more *no mores*. God is making all things new.

10

A New Heaven and a New Earth

One of my most valued possessions is a rock. It is actually a piece of concrete. It was given to me by a young man and his bride on the day I performed their wedding in 1990. One side is flat and painted white and red. The other side is rough and gray. I have had this rock for years, and have told many people about it. There is an important reason why I keep it.

The rock reminds me to never give up hoping that the world can be a better place. That hope is important. This world is often very troubling to me. I have prayed countless times for the world we live in. In church every Sunday I pray the Lord's Prayer with my congregation, and in that prayer we say: "Thy kingdom come, they will be done, on earth as it is in Heaven." And then we go back to the world, where we soon hear about another atrocious thing someone has done to someone else. Another child abducted and killed. 49 people murdered by drug lords. Women held captive by sexual predators. Children murdered in their classroom by a troubled young man with access to military weapons. The sacredness of human life continues to be violated.

It is troubling why God does not do more about this! In the same prayer we pray for our daily bread, and God gives us more than enough. We pray for our sins to be forgiven, and they are. We pray to be protected from temptation, and if we keep our heads on straight, he does that too. He even delivers us from the evil one, just as we pray he would do.

But when we pray "thy kingdom come, thy will be done on earth as it is in Heaven," the world continues to drift further away from God's will. It grows darker and more chaotic every day.

This is why I take time to look at my rock; my chunk of concrete, because it reminds me of what God can do about all this awful darkness. That rock was once a part of the Berlin wall, a barrier that once stood as a monument to the shattered human family. The Berlin wall was built in the middle of the city that divided East from West. But it also divided families, a country and the world. Our elders remember when that wall was built. Many of them fought in the war that created the wall. I used to hear about this wall as a kid. My parent's generation talked about this wall like it would always be there.

But in 1989, the Berlin wall was torn down. It was not a government decision that toppled it. It came down because people prayed. Young people on both sides of the wall started praying every night in churches in the east and the west, for this wall to come down. Those prayer meetings went on for over a year, and grew until tens of thousands of people were praying. And one night, after one of those prayer meetings, they came out with hammers and tore the wall down. No one tried to stop them. They just tore it down. The young man who gave me the rock was there. He was an American exchange student, doing a medical internship in West Berlin. He came home with a rather large piece of that wall, and in appreciation for my services at the time of his wedding, he chipped off a small piece and gave it to me.

I keep it because it reminds me that because God cares about us, the world has a chance. God can and will change the world. The Book of Revelation chapter 21 tells us about it. It tells us that a new Heaven and a new earth is coming, "*for the first heaven and the first earth had passed away . . .*" (Revelation 21:1b) Occasionally people wonder, why the scripture would speak of Heaven passing away. But what John appears to have seen is that the ancient division that has kept earth and Heaven apart has passed away. John sees a new reality, where earth and Heaven are one. He sees the heavenly city, called New Jerusalem, coming to earth, and a voice from the throne, which is the voice of God himself, announcing: *"Look! God's dwelling place is now among the people, and he will dwell with them. They will be his people, and God himself will be with them and be their God" (Revelation 21:3, NIV).*

That is the moment the prayers of all faithful people are answered. We will rejoice that God's kingdom has finally come to earth, and his will is done "on earth as it is in Heaven."

Until that day comes, the faithful arrive in Heaven and find themselves in a place very different from earth. Heaven is a place of justice, where all the wrongs of this world are made right. Heaven must exist, because God's justice demands it. You know as well as I do—we don't always get justice here. Sometimes evil has its way. Evil people do evil things and get away with it. But Heaven is where evil is eradicated and justice is truly done. 2 Peter 3:13 says, *"But according to his promise we are waiting for new Heavens and a new earth in which righteousness dwells."*

We are really going to love Heaven, because Heaven is a perfect place, where evil is gone and goodness and brotherhood prevail.

When we get to Heaven, we are not going to have to read in the paper about people killing each other. We are not going to turn on the TV (if they have it) and witness scenes of hate, division, cruelty. You will not need locks on your doors, and you won't have to worry about being out alone.

In Heaven we are going to treat each other like God wishes we would treat each other on earth. He wants us to treat each other like family. We are family. We are *his* family.

That is the point of one of the most well-known parables Jesus gave—The Parable of the rich man and Lazarus. The rich man, who is never named but who sometimes is given the name *Dives*, enjoyed luxury and opulence. In Jesus's day, people of wealth were admired as righteous. Their prosperity was thought of as a divine reward for their goodness.

Jesus turned that theology upside-down. He said when the rich man and Lazarus died, they both when to *Sheol*, the place of the dead. That place had two parts, one for the righteous and one for the unrighteous. The rich man went to the side of torment, but Lazarus went to the bosom of Abraham where he received comfort as a child of God. The rich man was not judged because he was rich. He was judged because he didn't treat Lazarus like a brother. Because the rich man and Lazarus were both Israelites, he should have taken Lazarus into his home. He should have used the resources he had to heal his wounds and help him get healthy, and find a job, and have a chance at a decent life. His disregard for a man he should have treated as a brother resulted in the wealthy man suffering God's judgment.

The failure of justice in our world is a symptom of a similar underlying indifference to each other. Before we can hurt, cheat, neglect or abuse another human being, we must forget that he or she is my brother or my sister. Once these fraternal ties are ignored, injustice become tolerable and even acceptable.

Our world is one in which we are more likely to focus on our differences: the haves and have not's, Main Street and Wall Street, black and white, Christian and non-Christian. Justice requires that we realign our perception of each other to reflect the deeper reality: all people, regardless of distinctions, are a part of a human family, which is the creation of our Heavenly Father. We are God's children. God is our Father, and we are brothers and sisters to one another. That we treat each other as family is God's will. When we fail, God's heart is the heart most broken. Any father (or mother) knows how true this is.

I was home one evening watching the kids, and I got them all bathed and ready for bed. They asked me if they could stay up a little late that night and play a game. They were so adorable as they begged and cajoled me. I could not resist their sweetness.

I said, "You know Mom wants you to go to bed now, but hey—it's Dad's rules tonight! So you can play one more game before you go to bed."

The little angels got all excited and ran to the play room and found the game that had the longest duration of play. They brought it to the living room and laid it out on the floor to play. Though I was in the next room, I could hear roll of the dice and the sound of my children laughing, talking and having a good time.

The bliss came to a sudden end when I heard one of them say "Hey—you cheated!"

"I did not cheat! You're just mad because I'm winning."

"You're winning because you keep cheating!"

Their voices got louder, and their accusations became more intense. And then I started to hear growling and snarling, and finally, a crash. When I went out to investigate, there were my two little angels, trying to kill each other. They were rolling around on the floor, scratching and hitting each other. My daughter was pounding my son with her fist. My son was trying to bite his sister. Their faces were locked in angry expressions. And it looked like they really intended to hurt each other. So I grabbed my son and pulled him off my daughter and picked them both up and carried them to their rooms, and while I was carrying them they were still trying to get at each other. I put them in their rooms and I shut the doors, and they were still screaming at each the through the wall. I shouted at their closed doors, "The two of you be quiet! I don't want to hear another sound out of you tonight!"

And when it was quiet, I went to the living room, and picked up all the pieces of the game they were playing and put it away. Then I went to the living room, sat down, and I started to cry. I cried pretty hard. I cried because these two little people that I love more than anything, were trying to hurt each other, over winning a game. I started thinking, where did I fail? What did I do wrong, that my 6 year old daughter and 4 year old son would behave that way?

But then I realized they behaved that way because they are like all the rest of us: they hate to lose, they cheat to win, and sometimes they forget they are members of the same family.

If you have ever had to go through the pain of seeing your children fight, or you are hurt today because your adult children don't get along, then you know what God feels like when he looks down on our world where we too easily forget that we are his children.

But there is a place where justice reigns. People who promote hate and violence will be judged, just like Jesus said. But those who stand for love and brotherhood will enter into a perfect place where hate and rage are eliminated and love, joy, and peace prevail. They already prevail in Heaven. But they will also someday prevail on earth, when earth and Heaven are one.

That day is coming. It was seen by John. God was giving us a glimpse of the final outcome, so we who have to live in this broken world can have hope. We can celebrate the victory here and now. Not with the swagger of people who say "My team is going to beat your team today," when they really don't know the outcome. We do know the outcome, because God has showed it to us.

Since I was raised in Chicago, I grew up as a Chicago sports fan. The 90's were exciting years for Chicago sports fans, because Michael Jordan's Bulls provided an NBA championship trophy to the city six of those ten years. But in the middle of those six years, Michael retired from basketball. He tried to play baseball. He tried even harder to act. The years without Michael Jordan were frustrating. Yet, I remained a fan, and watched every game.

During the interim of Jordan's retirement, the Bulls were locked in an intense struggle with the New York Knicks. Pivotal game six of that series was played on the evening an important meeting was held in our Church. Fortunately, I was ready for such situations. I was and owner of one of the most amazing devices of the 1990's—a video cassette recorder. My plan was to record the game on the VCR, attend the meeting, and when it was concluded, rush back home and watch the game as if it were live, except that I could fast-forward through the commercials and time-outs, cutting the time necessary for watching the game to a little over 12 minutes.

When the meeting concluded, I rushed home as planned, made a bowl of popcorn, and poured myself a soda. I sat down in my chair and prepared to push the "on" button on our old Magnavox console TV, which, because of its age, produced sound for a couple minutes before the picture. This was the cause of the unfortunate situation common to sports fans of my generation, which I experienced that night. The moment I turned pressed the "on" button, the announcer gave the final score of the game! "So the Bulls have defeated the Knicks 72-71 in Chicago." I spilled my popcorn trying to turn it off, but it was too late. I knew the final score. My evening was ruined.

But since I was there and had the free time, I decided to watch the game anyway, just to see how it all happened. I rewound the VHS tape to the beginning, played the video, and watched the game. I discovered that knowing the final score really changes one's experience of the game. In the first quarter, the Bulls fell behind by double digits to the Knicks, who were determined not to play a seventh game. Ordinarily, I would have been worried. But was not worried at all, because I knew the final score! With Michael Jordan retired (he was actually making a movie with Bugs Bunny at the time), the Bulls leaned on their other all-star player Scottie Pippen. In the second quarter, Pippen was injured, and limped to the Bulls locker room for treatment. If I had been watching live, I would have thought, "They can't win without Pippen." But I was not concerned at all, because I knew the final score. When the final quarter came, the Bulls were behind 71-69 with less than 5 seconds left. I didn't know how it was going to happen, but I knew what had to take place, all because I knew the final score. Scottie Pippen inbounded the ball, and two quick passes later, Croatian star Tony Kukoc launched a shot from well beyond the three-point line, *and nailed it!* The Bulls won that game, 72-71, exactly as I knew it had to be.

The book of Revelation is where God gives us the final score of history. When we get to the end, God wins. He already reigns in Heaven, and in the end, he will reign on earth too.

And living in that victory now, is one of the ways we make Heaven come to earth in us. When we're hurt, we forgive. When evil seems to have its way, we are patient. When we are trying to make a difference and we meet resistance, we persevere. We live with the joy of people who already have the victory, because we already have assurance about how history will unfold.

If you love justice you will love Heaven, because Heaven is a perfect place—of justice and brotherly love. If you love justice and love each other as brothers and sisters, you're really going to love it here too. Wherever God reigns, there his kingdom has come.

11

We Shall See God Face to Face

My three wonderful children called me up a week before Father's day and told me I needed to take that day off. As you get older, you learn to obey your children, so I took a vacation day so they could do to me whatever they planned to do.

They took me to a wonderful Italian restaurant I had never been to before. Note: when I say they *took* me, it just means they picked where we went. I still had to pay. Someday that will change—I hope.

But for Father's day they gave me a great gift. They gave me a book, called *The Ultimate book of Jokes* by Scott McNeely (Chronicle Books, 2011). I believe they gave it to me to upgrade the quality of my pulpit humor. It contains of 1500 jokes. Some of those jokes can actually be told from the pulpit. For example, this one found on page 15:

> **Two hunters are out in the woods when one of them collapses. He doesn't seem to be breathing and his eyes are glazed. The other guy whips out his phone and calls emergency services. He gasps, "My friend is dead! What can I do?"**
>
> **The operator says, "Calm down. I can help. First, let's make sure he's dead."**

There is silence, then a shot is heard. Back on the phone, the guy says, "Okay, now what?"

We spent the entire evening passing the book around reading the jokes, laughing so hard I thought we were going to get thrown out of the restaurant. But the customers close to us appreciated the humor as much as we did. Even after we left, we were still passing the book around, still giggling and laughing over the silly jokes. Eventually, as we were driving back home, I remember thinking, "How good must God be, to make life so joyful!"

Do you ever think about that? We sometimes talk too much about how difficult life is. Life is difficult sometimes, but it can also be intensely joyful, and happy, and full. That joy is made by God for us. How good must God be!

Our human experience gives us opportunity to see God, but almost always indirectly, through or within something we often think of as ordinary and mundane. We see God in laughter, and in the love of family and friends. We see him in Church. We see him in the Bible. We see him in the sacraments. We see him in the beauty of nature. We see him in the glory of the universe. We see him in each other, and hopefully, we see him in the mirror as well. We see God as he moves through our world, like the swaying tree branches allow us to see the invisible wind. Yet, there is more to come!

St. Paul said in 1 Corinthians 13: "*For now we see only a reflection as in a mirror; then we shall see face to face*" 1 Corinthians 13:12a. The best thing about Heaven is that we will finally see God face to face.

John MacArthur says "Heaven will provide us with that privilege—an undiminished, unwearied sight of His infinite glory and beauty, bringing us infinite and eternal delight." We may not be able to even imagine the difference. On earth we see God indirectly in the things God does and in the things he has made. But in Heaven we will see God in his full glory, face to face.

First, to see God means to be admitted into his presence. When we say we are going to see God, it doesn't mean just that we get to look at him, but that we get to have a direct relationship with him.

When you feel a little under the weather, you might call your physician's office and ask, "Would it be possible for me to see Dr. Smith today?" We don't mean simply that we want to look at him through the office window. We mean, *can I have an appointment with him?* Can I come to the office and meet with him; in person, face to face?

Seeing God means given the gift of being admitted to his presence. In Heaven we get to have a direct personal relationship with the One who made us. The Bible says that in Heaven there are so many people no one can number them. And yet God will have a direct, daily personal relationship with each one of us. How does that make you feel? Excited? Scared?

1 John 4:7-8 says, *"Beloved let us love one another, for love is of God, and everyone who loves is born of God and knows God. He who does not love does not know God, for God is love."* John does not describe God as a loving being. He says God is love itself. Love is the essence of who God is. Love was around before the world began, and love is the reason this world was made. God didn't make us because he needed people to worship him. He made us because in his greatness of heart, he needed to share the joys of the love he has always known. So he made us with one intent, that we might experience the joy of his loving nature. When we see God, we will find ourselves in the presence of love itself. How does that make you feel now? Still scared, or comforted?

Second, seeing God means being awestruck by his glory—by a direct experience of his greatness. After God confronted Job in the whirlwind, Job said, *"I had heard of thee by the hearing of the ear, but now my eye sees thee; therefore I despise myself, and repent in dust and ashes"* (Job 42:6).

When we get to Heaven, we will no longer have to understand his glory from lightning and mountains and roaring seas and constellations of stars. Instead our experience of him will be direct. His glory will be the very light in which we move, and by which we are transformed.

The book of Exodus gives us a preview of what that may be like. God called Moses to lead the people to their new destiny in the land of promise. But before they entered that land, they followed God in the desert, where they learned that God could be and had to be trusted in order for them to survive and prosper. When life became difficult for them, the people often complained to Moses. Moses occasionally found himself in a crisis of leadership, in which he himself began to doubt if he was the right one for the job. In one of these moments, described in Exodus 33, Moses pled that God, who up until then had appeared in a pillar of dust or fire, would give him and his recalcitrant people a clearer vision of him and of his intentions for them. In verse 18, Moses asks "Show me your glory," asking for the privilege of seeing God's face. God denied this request, but graciously offered Moses an alternative.

[19] And the Lord said, "I will cause all my goodness to pass in front of you, and I will proclaim my name, the Lord, in your presence. I will have mercy on whom I will have mercy, and I will have compassion on whom I will have compassion. [20] But," he said, "you cannot see my face, for no one may see me and live." [21] Then the Lord said, "There is a place near me where you may stand on a rock. [22] When my glory passes by, I will put you in a cleft in the rock and cover you with my hand until I have passed by. [23] Then I will remove my hand and you will see my back; but my face must not be seen" (Exodus 33:19-23, NIV).

God instructed Moses to make two stone tablets, and ascend Mt. Sinai. There God wrote down the basic commandments of the law, while keeping Moses hidden in rocky cleft a short distance away. When God departed, Moses looked and saw a brief glimpse of God's "back." The result is documented in Exodus 34:

29 When Moses came down from Mount Sinai with the two tablets of the covenant law in his hands, he was not aware that his face was radiant because he had spoken with the Lord. 30When Aaron and all the Israelites saw Moses, his face was radiant, and they were afraid to come near him. 31 But Moses called to them; so Aaron and all the leaders of the community came back to him, and he spoke to them. 32 Afterward all the Israelites came near him, and he gave them all the commands the Lord had given him on Mount Sinai (Exodus 34:29-32, NIV).

The glory of God had "rubbed off" on Moses, even though he only saw God's back. But in Heaven, we will see God's face! That moment will be truly transforming!

Finally, seeing God means being comforted by his grace. Again and again the psalmists cry out to God, for example in Psalm 27 (verses 7-9) David says,

Hear, O Lord, when I cry aloud,
be gracious to me and answer me!
. . . do not hide your face from me.

"Hide not thy face from me," is the same as saying, "Be gracious to me!" This means that seeing the face of God is going to be a sweet and comforting experience. If God shows his face, we are helped. If he turns his face away, we are dismayed.

When we get to Heaven we are going to see the face of God. It will not be an angry face or disappointed face. Not a face that makes us feel we didn't achieve much. God's face will be the face of a parent whose child has been lost, and then was found.

When I pastored the church north of Grand Rapids, I had the occasion to go down to Blodgett hospital, and see a young couple in the church who had a baby. I always enjoyed that kind of hospital visit. So I remember I parked in the parking garage, and went in, and took the elevator up to the fourth floor, the maternity floor. And when the elevator doors opened I became witness to this beautiful scene. A mother was standing near the nurses' station holding her baby. She was standing facing the elevator, and holding the baby up on her shoulder. And behind her, three nurses were going crazy over this baby. They were making those faces and noises we are not allowed to make except in the presence of an infant.

I quickly assumed that, what was happening was, this mother had given birth to this baby in the hospital, and the baby was now about 6 months old, so she came back to show off her baby. The most touching part of the whole scene was the expression on this young mother's face. That mother looked so proud, so happy, so full of love for her baby. I thought, this must be the most beautiful baby ever born.

The baby was wearing a little white dress and a bonnet, and was facing away from me. But because of the fuss they were making, and because of the beauty of the mother's expression, I had to get a look at this baby's face. So I walked all the way around the nurse's station and, as I did, I turned my head, and looked.

She was a Down's Syndrome baby. The baby had the pronounced features of a baby with what used to be called "mongolism," and which today is still considered a birth defect.

But the amazing thing about that is, the expression on the baby's mother's face said that that child was nothing other than beautiful. The mother's face said her baby was perfect. And I am sure that in her mother's eyes, she always has been.

Of all the things that make Heaven to beautiful place, seeing God face to face is the most sublime, the most wonderful! For all eternity, we will see the face of the one whose love has taken us defective sinners and transformed us to perfection. In the gaze of perfect love and grace, we will be totally transformed, and live in eternal joy.

12

A Peaceful Journey's End

T he Danish Philosopher Soren Kierkegaard, wrote about a mythical little town inhabited exclusively by ducks. Every Sunday morning, the ducks would waddle out of their houses and waddle down Main Street to their church. They would waddle into the sanctuary and squat in their favorite pews. Then the duck choir would waddle in and take its place in the choir loft. Then the duck minister would come forward and open the duck Bible and read to them. He would tell them: "Brother and sister Ducks! God has given you wings! With wings you can fly! You can soar like eagles. No walls can confine you! No fences can hold you! God has given you wings and you can fly like birds!" All the ducks in the congregation would shout "Amen!"

Then, these ducks would all get up and waddle out the door, quacking about the wonderful sermon they heard that day. And then they would waddle all the way home.

Preachers love that story because it is a non-threatening, yet still convicting story about how we must live our faith. In church, we like to talk about how faith is not just a mental acceptance of the truth. Faith is the wings of the Christian life. Why waddle when you are able to fly?

So, in the Church we spend a lot of time teaching people how to use their wings; how to live out what we believe in practical ways. We preach sermons and have seminars on how to be a Christian parent, how to handle your money, how to have a happy marriage, how to witness, how to overcome addictions, how to pray, how to worship, and almost everything else you can think of about how to live out your faith, except one. We don't talk much about how to die.

That is odd for two reasons. First, dying is something every one of us will do. The universality of death should be obvious. We spend a good portion of our lives pretending that it is not going to happen to us, but it will happen anyway. Woody Allen once said, "I don't want to achieve immortality through my work. I want to achieve it by not dying!" As much as we might wish Woody's statement was more than humor, we know deep down it is not. All of us will someday die. You will die. Your children will die. Your neighbors, your friends; the rich, the poor, Christian, Muslim, and Jew—every one of us without exception, will die. But the other reason I am surprised we don't give more instruction about how to die is because of the unique perspective we Christians have on death. We die "in faith." We die as people who go forth to live forever.

This means that death does not "happen to" the Christian. We can and should prepare for dying, and, if we can, make choices ahead of time about how we die.

The people of the Bible thought of dying as the last act of service we will get to do for God here on earth. And they put a lot of thought into how they did it. They blessed their children, gave final instructions, and praised God for his wonderful care over the years. Our goal should be, to do what they did; to choose how we leave this world, and to die in faith.

First, make your final arrangements as early as possible. Those arrangements include a will, funeral arrangements and a living will. A living will is a legal document that you can use to express how you would like to be treated if you cannot speak for yourself. It is also known as an advance directive, health care directive, or a physician's directive. Your living will tells your health care providers and your family about how much life-sustaining treatment you wish to receive in case you become incapacitated and cannot express your preferences when necessary. It takes a burdensome decision out of your family's hands at a difficult time, and gives them assurance about how you wish to be cared for medically. An attorney can help you with the tasks of making a will and a living will. Your local Funeral Director can help you prearrange your funeral or memorial service. In spite of ethical questions raised about some funeral practices, my experience has been that almost all funeral directors truly want to serve dying person and their family. You should never be reluctant to talk to a funeral director. You can never be too early, but you can be too late!

Second, make plans for your care as you enter the dying process. Death is not always a process; sometimes it comes suddenly and without warning. Some people prefer it that way. But if you are told you are sick with a disease or condition that is considered terminal, don't simply wait to die. Take control of your comfort and quality of life. One way you can do this is by enrolling in hospice care.

Hospice is one of the most under-utilized medical services available today. This is often because enrolling in hospice care requires us to accept that we are in our last days. Yet, hospice does not require that we give up hope. Hospice simply shifts the goals of care from life-prolonging medical treatment to care centered around comfort and quality of life. Hospice helps you face your last days with as little pain as possible. Your hospice care team will help you sleep better, eat better, and assist you in facing your death without profound fear or sadness. And when you enroll is hospice, Medicare and many private insurance policies cover your medical treatment 100% with no deductible or copay.

If you have enrolled in hospice and you wish to pursue a new a potentially curing treatment, you may revoke your hospice benefit and engage in treatment. It happens. But even if your disease follows its typical course, your quality of life will be better than if your face your last days alone.

Planning for the day you die also involves seeking assurance about the past. It means taking time to knowing that your sins are forgiven, and that the moment you see God, you will stand before him free from sin, by his own mercy. It means developing or maintaining confidence in God's love when the time comes. Often, the fears we have are not about eternity, but about the process of dying itself. Those fears are natural, because we are always apprehensive about things we've never done before. Yet, we can continue to have the same confidence that the grace of God, which directed our steps through life, will guide us through life's final journey. Even as you die, the love of God will hold you, and will not let you go. With that confidence, you can make your last days, or even your last hours, a time full of special memories and blessings for you and your family.

If you know you are dying, kiss your children and grandchildren and tell them you love them. Give them permission to stay with you if they want, but make sure they know it's ok for them to go home, eat and rest. If they tell you they don't want you to die alone, remind them that you're not alone. Tell them that God is right there with you, because he will be there.

Finally, to die in faith means to look forward to a blessed future. That's what the senior saints of the Bible did. The saints of the scripture often died not being able to see the fulfillment of what they were promises. Abraham was promised so many descendants they would be like the stars in the sky. Yet he only got to see the beginning—the birth of his son Isaac. He had to trust God for the future fulfillment of God's promise—and so do we.

My friend Bill loves to tell the story of his mother's wonderful death. His mother lived her entire life in faith—she was a Sunday School teacher in the Baptist Church all her life. And when it came time for her to die, she was ready. Her first decision was that she was going to die in her home in her bed, not in some hospital room where her family would be uncomfortable. On the day she died, she gathered Bill and the other children around her bed and told each one of them what she thought was special about them. She told the little ones to listen to their Mommies and Daddies, and she told the older ones to love their little ones every second, because there was so little time in life to waste.

She told them stories of how God took care of her when she was young and had very little. She told them to be grateful for everything they have, especially each other. She told them she was going to a beautiful place, and she looked forward to seeing them there. Then she shut her eyes. And her breathing began to slow down. And every time her breathing stopped, the family would wait . . . . then she would start breathing again. She would stop . . . they would wait . . . and then she would start breathing again . . . After doing this for several hours, just a few minutes before she actually passed, Bill says that his mother opened her eyes, looked around, and with genuine disappointment said, "Am I still here?"

Bill loves to tell that story. And even though he tells it frequently, people love to hear it. I still tell it all the time myself. Because it's message is so wonderful.

Because, to die in faith means to die as someone going forth to live! We've been waddling around here on earth like grounded ducks for a long time! Our dying day is the day we get to extend our wings and fly!

Finding Assurance about Heaven

13

The Senior Saints I serve as chaplain know that I am not terribly fond of dressing in a suit and tie. I do dress up when necessary; especially for Sunday chapel services or for a special event— and many times, that event is the funeral of a departed brother or sister. Because of this, people often approach me with grave concern when they see me dressed in a suit and tie in the middle of the week. It's actually somewhat discouraging. When I dress up in a nice suit and a sharp tie, I want people to say, "Oh, how nice you look today!" When the folks at my facility see me come to the office dressed in a tie, they say, "Who died?"

I came to the office dressed in a suit and tie on the day I performed the funeral for Gerald, a man who died rather suddenly earlier in that week. When I was getting my morning coffee, one of the servers in our restaurant saw how I was dressed and asked, "Do you have a funeral today?"

"Yes," I said.

"Who is it?" she asked.

"It's Gerald. He died of a heart attack a few days ago, and his service will be at 11:00 AM today."

The server's expression turned very sad. A single tear trickled out of her eye as she said," Oh, I loved Gerald. And I didn't get to say goodbye!"

I immediately tried to offer reassurance. I said, "Don't worry, you'll see him again. You'll see him in Heaven."

She said, "I hope I get to see him in Heaven. I know Gerald is in Heaven, and I hope I get to go there too."

As she walked away, I called to her, "Do you trust in Jesus?"

She said, "I sure do!"

I said, "Then I'll see you in Heaven!"

She responded, "I hope so."

This understanding about our entry into Heaven is all too common, and sadly mistaken. We should have more than mere hope about our eternal home. We should have assurance. We should live our lives and our deaths in complete assurance that when our life is over, we will celebrate in God's Heavenly kingdom in all of the ways this book describes.

I want to tell you in the simplest as possible terms how to find this assurance. Though it is the central affirmation of the entire great Scriptural narrative, it can be summed up in two simple words:

Trust Jesus.

Notice that I did not say, "trust Jesus and go to church." It is not "trust Jesus and read the Bible." It is not even "trust Jesus and live a good life." There are important reasons for going to church, reading the Bible, and living a good life. But entry into Heaven has nothing to do with any of these things. If we come to believe that going to Heaven has anything to do with what we do, we immediately make assurance impossible. If Heaven depends on us, hope is the best we can do. People who hold this theological mindset—and there are many—regard it as arrogant to think that you can *know* you are going to Heaven. Yet, our assurance about Heaven is not based on anything we have done at all.

God wants us to have assurance. We gain assurance by simply trusting in Jesus. We get to Heaven because of what God has done for us (in Jesus), not by what we do for God. What we do for God is called religion. What God has done for us is salvation.

While serving as a hospice chaplain, I was called to a local nursing home to visit a hospice patient in the middle of the night. His name was Sonny. I went to Sonny's room and met him and asked him what he needed. He said he knew he was dying, and he wanted the last rites. So I said, "Oh, are you Catholic?" And he looked away, then back, and he nodded his head. So I said, "Hold on a minute."

I went back to the nurse' station and I told the nurse who was there "Sonny wants the last rites. You need to call a catholic priest." She smiled and said, "Sonny's not catholic." And she looked in the chart and showed me where he had checked "no preference" on his application.

So then I realized what was happening. Sonny was facing his mortality, and he was trying to cover all the bases. So I went back to Sonny's room and I performed the best last rites I could make up on the spot. Sonny started crossing himself or doing the Macarena—I don't know which. And then I said, "Sonny, do you trust in Jesus?" He said, "Yes I do." I said, "Sonny you don't need to worry. If you trust in Jesus, he's your savior. You don't have to worry about your future. He'll get you there!"

You can hear God's desire that we have assurance about eternity in many the things Jesus said about Heaven. For example, in John chapter 14, he said, "Do not let your hearts be troubled. You believe in God; believe also in me. My Father's house has many rooms; if that were not so, would I have told you that I am going there to prepare a place for you? And if I go and prepare a place for you, I will come back and take you to be with me that you also may be where I am. You know the way to the place where I am going."

Thomas said to him, "Lord, we don't know where you are going, so how can we know the way?"

Jesus answered, "I am the way and the truth and the life. No one comes to the Father except through me" (John 14:1-6).

It is unfortunate that, for some, verse 6 has come to mean, "Only those people who adhere to the religion that developed around Jesus will go to Heaven." This is not what Jesus meant at all! He meant that he was going there to open the door, hold it open for anyone who, through trust in him, wishes to use it. The entire world is invited. Trust is the way.

You can't die in faith if you have doubts about eternity. The Bible teaches that those who trust in Jesus should have assurance as we face our mortality. It's not about our own goodness; it's about the goodness of God and of Jesus Christ our savior. If you trust Jesus, you can die knowing that by the mercy of God, your place in God's kingdom is as secure as God's love for you.

Though I have always understood this concept as a Christian, still my heart struggled with feelings of unworthiness. While serving as a young associate pastor and a large church, I often felt overwhelmed with people's expectations. I felt even more overwhelmed by what I thought were God's expectations. I always wondered: *will I ever be worthy? Will I ever feel worthy?*

These nagging self-doubts let me to take a course in clinical pastoral education at Bronson Methodist Hospital in Kalamazoo Michigan. About halfway through the semester, I shared these feelings with my supervisor. I asked him how much I had to do, how perfect I need to be before I feel good enough for God. His answer seemed very odd at first. He said, "You learn that from your children."

Over the next several days, I paid special attention to our two year old daughter, waiting for her to reveal this esoteric wisdom. However, she did not seem to be interested in my quest at all. She just wanted to play with her stuffed Elmo, and get into various kinds of mischief.

Friday morning of that week, our senior pastor asked me to visit a member of our church who was struggling to recover from heart surgery. I drove to the hospital in Kalamazoo still thinking about when, if ever, I would feel good enough for God. I was also thinking about my daughter, and what she could possibly teach me about all this.

When I arrived in the hospital parking lot, I stopped the car and turned off the engine. Then I had a life-changing thought. In one holy moment it occurred to me that I have been Leah's father for over two years, and not once during all that time had I ever asked myself if she was good enough for me. Oh, I was aware when she was good and when she was not so good. But I had never entertained a thought about whether I should keep her, or take her back to the hospital and trade her in on a better child. It is not that I have judged her worthy of my love either. I simply have never thought about it.

I learned, from my children, that a father's love is not based on anything that children do. A father loves his child because she is his child.

That's what Jesus meant when he told us to call God "Father." That God is our father has to do with the fact that he made us, but so much more to do with the fact that he adores us; and that his love for us is not based on anything we do or anything we are. We are his children. That's all we will ever need to be.

So the next time someone asks you if you know you were going to Heaven, you may answer with a grateful and most assured "Yes!" The assurance of Heaven comes from knowing that God is our Father and that he has done everything that needs to be done for us to enter the place that gives us a blessed eternity. Jesus himself is holding open the door.

Appendix
The Heaven on
Earth Study Guide

I have included this study guide because I believe that, while Heaven is a wonderful and perfect place, the things that make Heaven the place that it is are available to us in great measure here on earth. God's intention is not that we be miserable on earth so we can be more joyful in Heaven. Our misery here on earth is often the result of our failure to understand that the things Heaven offers us are there for us now.

For example, chapter one of this book describes Heaven as a place of eternal rest. The corresponding Bible study is about the concept of rest in the Scripture, particularly for the Old Testament people of God. It helps us understand the Biblical affirmation that life is a gift from God, and invites us to embrace rest as an affirmation of the faithfulness of God's care.

Chapters two and three of this book talks about the blessed reunion we will enjoy in Heaven with those who have gone before us. Because we know Heaven is essentially relational, we should be more diligent about maintaining good relationships with our family and friends here on earth. Relationships characterized by love and grace enhance our quality of life in a way that previews the great reunion of the heavenly people of God made up of people of all nations, races, and languages.

In this study guide you will find a Biblical examination of food as a form of celebration. You'll find a study that teaches that our ultimate home is not a place but a person. The study that parallels the chapter of the book of about seeing God face to face gives suggestions about the places where we can look for God while we live here on earth. And the final study will guide you in making preparations for the journey that leads us to Heaven. It's called, "Living into Eternal Life.

The point, of course, is that it is not necessary to die to experience the joys of Heaven. Our gracious and wonderful God has given us the privilege of enjoying "Heaven on earth."

Sabbath Rest

Modern life is stressful, and that stress may be killing us. Read this:

Stress is one of the leading causes of illness in the United States. Indeed, nearly 66 percent of all signs and symptoms presented in doctors' offices in the U.S. are stress induced. [1]

On a scale of 1-10 (10 being the worst), how stressed do you feel right now?

Name the major sources of stress in your life:

People cope with stress in a variety of ways. Some of those ways are self-defeating or even unhealthy. Alcohol and drug abuse are obvious examples. Can you think of others?

---

[1] http://personalliberty.com/2010/02/23/how-stress-is-killing-us-and-10-things-you-can-do-about-it/

Philippians 4:6-7 (NIV)

Do not be anxious about anything, but in every situation, by prayer and petition, with thanksgiving, present your requests to God. And the peace of God, which transcends all understanding, will guard your hearts and your minds in Christ Jesus.

Rewrite this passage here in your own words:

If we have excessive stress, we can either eliminate some of the sources of stress, or develop a greater capacity for coping with it. Paul's advice in Philippians is directed toward the latter. He encourages us to engage in activity that strengthens our trust in God. As our trust in God increases, so does our ability to cope with the pressured inherent to modern life.

In nature, a sinkhole is created when atmospheric pressure upon the surface of the earth is not equalized by water pressure within an underground cave. In dry seasons, the underground well can empty, leaving a void. The atmospheric pressure from above forces the soil down, creating a sinkhole. A sinkhole does not "fall in;" it is "pushed down" because it lacks equalizing pressure from below.

Many Christians become spiritual sinkholes, because they lack internal spiritual strength to cope with the stresses of life. The Sabbath Principle is designed to help us do on earth what people in Heaven always do: celebrate the bounteous provision of God for our lives. Sabbath teaches us to place our trust in God, and not in ourselves.

Genesis 2:2 (NIV)

By the seventh day God had finished the work he had been doing; so on the seventh day he rested from all his work. Then God blessed the seventh day and made it holy, because on it he rested from all the work of creating that he had done.

Though Sabbath is a feature of Christian and Jewish theology, it is the claim of these faiths that the origin of Sabbath precedes both Jesus and the Jewish law. Sabbath is a natural rhythm, woven into the fabric of creation itself.

What other rhythms have you noticed in creation?

Ways of Experiencing Strengthening Through Rest

1. **Respect the balance of Work and Rest**

How many hours do you spend in the following activities:

1. Work:
2. Service to God:
3. Rest:
4. Play:
5. Worship:

Are you satisfied with these proportions? Do they reflect a balanced approach to life?

What unique challenges does your vocation present you that make it difficult to take time off? Can you do anything about those challenges?

Read the Story of Manna found in Exodus 16, and answer these questions about what you read:

What kind of environment were the Israelites living in?

What were they complaining about?

What was God's response to the people's complaint?

What happened if people kept the manna overnight?

How many days a week did God give the manna?

There was no manna on the Sabbath day; yet the people did not go hungry. Why not?

What happened when the people kept the manna overnight on the Sabbath Day?

What was God trying to teach his people?

Manna was not a random, natural substance. If it were, it could not have appeared in the pattern described in the Scripture. Manna was a miraculous expression of God's provision, given in such a way so that the Israelite community, struggling to find its identity, would learn to trust in God.

Sabbath is a principle, not a law. A legalistic approach to Sabbath (in which keeping the Sabbath is defined by what you do not do) misses the point. Why?

2. **Get a Good Night's Sleep**

Psalm 4:6-8 (NIV)

Many, Lord, are asking, "Who will bring us prosperity?"
Let the light of your face shine on us.
Fill my heart with joy
when their grain and new wine abound.

In peace I will lie down and sleep,
for you alone, Lord,
make me dwell in safety.

What is King David stressed about?

Why is David able to sleep?

David responds to the stresses of leadership with an attitude of humility and trust. Knowing that everything is in God's hands, he is able to lie down in peace and sleep.

How would you rate your current sleep habits?

ZZZZ— I get at least 8 hours of uninterrupted sleep almost every night.

ZZZ— I generally sleep well, with only an occasional disruption.

ZZ— I get a good night's sleep 1 or 2 nights a week.

Z— I have all kinds of trouble going to sleep or staying asleep

0 Z's— Sorry, what was that? I must have dozed off.

Approaching sleep as an expression of Sabbath can help you find quality rest. Prior to going to bed, you may

- Pray, giving all your worries into God's care.
- Refuse to think of the things that are bothering you.
- Think about how much God loves you.
- Refuse to do "mental" work—planning the next day, pouring over problems.
- Remind yourself that God is taking care of everything.

If you find yourself feeling drowsy most days, falling asleep at your desk, in dark rooms or at traffic lights, you should consult a physician who specializes in sleep problems. You may have sleep apnea, a common and serious sleep deprivation disorder, in which you actually stop breathing during deep sleep, and partially wake up to resume breathing. Often a spouse is more aware of these patterns than you are. But only a sleep study can diagnoge the presence of sleep apnea, and it is treatable by losing weight and the use of a C-PAP machine.

3. Do a "Field Study" of God's goodness

When was your last vacation? Where did you go? Was is a time of stress or rest?

Matthew 6:25–31 (NIV):

Therefore I tell you, do not worry about your life, what you will eat or drink; or about your body, what you will wear. Is not life more than food, and the body more than clothes? Look at the birds of the air; they do not sow or reap or store away in barns, and yet your Heavenly Father feeds them. Are you not much more valuable than they? Can any one of you by worrying add a single hour to your life? And why do you worry about clothes? See how the flowers of the field grow. They do not labor or spin. Yet I tell you that not even Solomon in all his splendor was dressed like one of these. If that is how God clothes the grass of the field, which is here today and tomorrow is thrown into the fire, will he not much more clothe you—you of little faith?

Is this a command or a suggestion?

What specifically does Jesus want us to see in nature?

How is worry related to the smallness of our faith?

How does observation of the natural world strengthen our faith?

How often do you experience nature? How can you increase your time in God's created world?

Study 2

Love is a Verb

Besides Jesus, who are you most looking forward to seeing in Heaven?

Who would you like to spend a day with in Heaven?

1 Corinthians 13:8-13 (NIV)

Love never fails. But where there are prophecies, they will cease; where there are tongues, they will be stilled; where there is knowledge, it will pass away. For we know in part and we prophesy in part, but when completeness comes, what is in part disappears. When I was a child, I talked like a child, I thought like a child, I reasoned like a child. When I became a man, I put the ways of childhood behind me. For now we see only a reflection as in a mirror; then we shall see face to face. Now I know in part; then I shall know fully, even as I am fully known.

And now these three remain: faith, hope and love. But the greatest of these is love.

Think about this quote by John Wesley:

Holy solitaries' is a phrase no more consistent with the Gospel than holy adulterers. The Gospel of Christ knows no religion but social; no holiness, but social holiness."

What do you think Wesley meant?

What words might we substitute for "solitaries" today?

Evangelical Christianity emphasizes the need for an individual making a decision for Christ, as opposed to the idea that we are saved by affiliating with a Church through membership. While this emphasis is important, it is helpful to remember that an authentic decision for Christ brings one into a relationship with other Christians.

Implied in 1 Corinthians 13:13 is the idea that Heavenly life is a more perfect expression of earthly life. If earthly life is social, heavenly life is more social. We know fully, and we are fully known. That implies that the barriers that keep people apart are removed, and we are able to relate to each other (and to God) each without obstacles like shame, guilt, fear, hurt, sin, etc.

John 13:34-35 (NIV)

"A new command I give you: Love one another. As I have loved you, so you must love one another. By this everyone will know that you are my disciples, if you love one another."

Why does Jesus call this a "new" command?

The purpose of the 10 Commandments was to give the Israelite people a distinct identity. They were to be devoted to only one God, and to the specific moral and social order described by Him. By connecting his words to the ancient Mosaic commandments, Jesus is telling us that brotherly love among his people is more than a good idea. Love is essential to the nature of following him. It is the distinct mark that identifies us as his disciples.

Because Christians are the redeemed community on earth, healthy relationships are essential to experiencing Heaven on earth.

Make a list of the things that make relationships difficult.

Name Three Characteristics of Healthy Relationships

T _____

F _____

R _____

Trust Involves:
>Honesty in communication.
>Being able to say how you feel without consequences.
>Being able to admit mistakes; forgiving and being forgiven.

Freedom involves:
>Giving others freedom to be different from you.
>Acceptance
>Not judging others

Respect involves:
>Regarding others are people of God's family
>Regulating your own speech and behavior toward others
>Valuing other's opinions

Choose one of these three areas to work on or practice in the next few weeks, and see if it makes a difference.

Study 3

I've Got a Mansion

In your mind, picture a house, or draw one below:

Why did you draw the house this way?

A house can be a ranch, a duplex, a teepee or an igloo. What do all houses have in common?

John 14:1-3 (NIV)

"Do not let your hearts be troubled. You believe in God; believe also in me. My Father's house has many rooms; if that were not so, would I have told you that I am going there to prepare a place for you? And if I go and prepare a place for you, I will come back and take you to be with me that you also may be where I am.

In this scripture, the word "house" in the Greek is "oikia" (pronounced oy-kee'-ah) and means "household" and by extension "family". The word "mansions" is "mone" (pronounced 'mon-ay') and means "residence" (the act of residing or the place in which one resides).

Compare the following translations. Which do you like best?

KJV— *In my Father's house are many mansions*
NIV— *My Father's house has many rooms*
AMP— *In My Father's house there are many dwelling places (homes).*
NLT— *There is more than enough room in my Father's home*
MSG— *There is plenty of room for you in my Father's home*

The King James version of the Bible uses *mansion* because it borrows from the latin translation of the word monay. The contemporary translations shy away from the idea that we should be pursuing a wealthy eternity.

The big debate about the use of the term mansion is only part of the issue of correct understanding of these verses.

1) **Eternity is a gift of God, not a reward.** In some parts of the world (England, for example), the place where the Vicar lives is still called the Mansion (or sometimes, Manse). The designation of the house as mansion has nothing to do with its opulence, but refers to the fact that it is provided freely as the place for the Vicar to live.

There is no evidence in scripture that our good works enhance the opulence of our Heavenly manse. Rather, the fact that it is called a mansion may have more to do with the fact that it is a place, provided by God, in which we live forever.

2) **Our Home in Heaven is an expression of the Love of Christ for us.** Jesus gives us a home because he wants us to live with him. Notice how Jesus said *"If I go . . . I will come."* John 14:2 is accessing 1st century Jewish wedding tradition.

When a young Jewish man saw a woman he wished to marry, he (often with his father) would go to the father of the prospective bride and make an arrangement. When this contract was agreed to, and the price for the bride paid, the couple was considered to be married. The groom and his father would then return home and prepare a place for the he and his bride to live. Depending on his resources, it may be a separate home, or a room added to the existing house. The process of "preparing a place" often took up to a year to complete. When the new place was ready, the groom could go claim his bride.

The groom would arrive often at midnight in a mock "abduction," and bring his bride to their new home. The two families would celebrate joyfully the union of their two families. A first century Jewish wedding celebration often went on for days!

Knowing the wedding traditions of the biblical people helps us to understand the logic of Jesus' statement in the gospel of John: "Because I go . . . I will return." Many people leave without ever coming back. Why does the assurance of Jesus' return come from the fact that he is going away?

The wedding tradition explains this easily: We are Jesus' bride. Having bought us and redeemed us by his own blood, he has now gone to prepare a place for us to live. It would be unthinkable that the groom would not return for the bride he has paid for.

Thus, the home we have in Heaven is a symbol of His desire to be live with us eternally.

Study 4

A Heavenly Banquet

What was your favorite holiday? Did it involve a big meal? What was served?

How does your church use eating as a form of celebration?

What food do you hope to see on the heavenly banquet table?

Revelation 19:6-9 (NIV)

Then I heard what sounded like a great multitude, like the roar of rushing waters and like loud peals of thunder, shouting:
"Hallelujah!
For our Lord God Almighty reigns.
Let us rejoice and be glad
and give him glory!
For the wedding of the Lamb has come,
and his bride has made herself ready.

⁸Fine linen, bright and clean,
was given her to wear."
(Fine linen stands for the righteous acts of God's holy people.)
Then the angel said to me, "Write this: Blessed are those who are invited to the wedding supper of the Lamb!" And he added, "These are the true words of God."

Once again, John uses 1ˢᵗ Century Jewish marriage to give people an understanding of eternity.

1) **The Betrothal:** The first step was the establishment of the marriage covenant that bound the man and woman together as husband and wife.
2) **The Claiming of the Bride:** The Groom would come and "abduct" his bride from her father's house and bring her to his house or his father's.
3) **The Wedding Banquet:** Once the marriage had been consummated by the bride and groom, the wedding guests would feast and make merry for seven days.

Early Christians used this traditional liberally to understand the plan of salvation.

1) **The Betrothal:** Jesus came to our home, established a binding covenant with us that made us his bride. He then returned to his home, to prepare a place for us in his father's house. I am jealous for you with a godly jealousy. I promised you to one husband, to Christ, so that I might prese*nt you as a pure virgin to him.* 2 Corinthians 11:2 (NIV)
2) **The Claiming of the Bride:** Jesus returns (like a thief in the night) to claim his bride. His people are abducted out of the world, and taken to his father's house.
3) **The Wedding Banquet of the Lamb is held.** It is a joyful even; a heavenly meal, celebrating God's final victory and the consummation of all history. It is a celebration that will have no end.

In the Church, we have a celebration that serves as the "appetizer" to the heavenly banquet. It is called Holy Communion or The Lord's Supper.

1 Corinthians 11:17-26 (NIV)

[17] *In the following directives I have no praise for you, for your meetings do more harm than good.* [18] *In the first place, I hear that when you come together as a church, there are divisions among you, and to some extent I believe it.* [19] *No doubt there have to be differences among you to show which of you have God's approval.* [20] *So then, when you come together, it is not the Lord's Supper you eat,* [21] *for when you are eating, some of you go ahead with your own private suppers. As a result, one person remains hungry and another gets drunk.* [22] *Don't you have homes to eat and drink in? Or do you despise the church of God by humiliating those who have nothing? What shall I say to you? Shall I praise you? Certainly not in this matter!**

[23] *For I received from the Lord what I also passed on to you: The Lord Jesus, on the night he was betrayed, took bread,* [24] *and when he had given thanks, he broke it and said, "This is my body, which is for you; do this in remembrance of me."* [25] *In the same way, after supper he took the cup, saying, "This cup is the new covenant in my blood; do this, whenever you drink it, in remembrance of me."* [26] *For whenever you eat this bread and drink this cup, you proclaim the Lord's death until he comes.*

What is Paul so upset about?

Christian worship, in which Holy Communion is the highest expression, is intended to be an anticipatory experience; literally a preview of Heaven. In early Christian worship, people gathered to celebrate what was coming. Some worshiped in the morning on the first day of the week, and others worshipped in the evening, or at other times. Their worship typically began with a shared community meal, called an Agape Feast, which was followed by Holy Communion.

The Agape Feast died out in the fourth century. After that time, worship became more formalized, and the focus of communion shifted to become a memorial to the death of Jesus.

What was it about the agape meal that caused early Christians to regard it as worship?

The divisions that troubled the Corinthian Church indicated that they had forgotten the actual purpose of the Agape meal. Food exists to nourish our bodies, but if this is the only purpose, there is no need to share a common meal in the Church. That kind of meal is a form of spiritual celebration.

How does your family use food to celebrate?

Should Holy Communion be more celebrative? How could it be without losing sight of its importance?

How does your church use food to celebrate the victory of Jesus?

Food is a Binding Agent of Community

Acts 2:46-47 (NIV)

[46] *Every day they continued to meet together in the temple courts. They broke bread in their homes and ate together with glad and sincere hearts, [47] praising God and enjoying the favor of all the people. And the Lord added to their number daily those who were being saved.*

Why does the author of Acts give such a prominent place to the breaking of bread?

Why does eating together solidify friendships?

Besides your family, who do you eat with regularly?

Does your church celebrate enough?

Assignment: Identify some people you do not know very well, and invite them over for dinner.

Study 5

A Glorious New Body

Name something you could do 10 years ago that you can no longer do.

Make a list of the things you do not like about getting older.

What age were you when you first noticed that you were aging? What was the first sign?

Philippians 3:20-21 (NIV)

[20] *But our citizenship is in Heaven. And we eagerly await a Savior from there, the Lord Jesus Christ,* [21] *who, by the power that enables him to bring everything under his control, will transform our lowly bodies so that they will be like his glorious body.*

It is certain that our earthly existence would be happier if our physical bodies were not subject to the effects of time. The assurance the scripture gives us of a new body that will remain youthful and energetic for all eternity is intended be a source of joy to all.

What does Paul mean when he says "our citizenship is in Heaven?"

Why does Paul describe our bodies as "lowly?"

Why does Paul describe Jesus' body as "glorious?"

How you feel knowing that someday you will be "glorious," as Jesus is?

Luke 24:36-43 (NIV)

[36] *While they were still talking about this, Jesus himself stood among them and said to them, "Peace be with you."*

[37] *They were startled and frightened, thinking they saw a ghost.* [38] *He said to them, "Why are you troubled, and why do doubts rise in your minds?* [39] *Look at my hands and my feet. It is I myself! Touch me and see; a ghost does not have flesh and bones, as you see I have."*

[40] *When he had said this, he showed them his hands and feet.* [41] *And while they still did not believe it because of joy and amazement, he asked them, "Do you have anything here to eat?"* [42] *They gave him a piece of broiled fish,* [43] *and he took it and ate it in their presence.*

What was the disciples' initial reaction to seeing Jesus?

Why do you think people are superstitious about ghosts?

How did Jesus prove to his disciples that he was not a ghost?

Why did Jesus eat a piece of the broiled fish?

Why did Jesus invite the disciples to examine his hands and feet?

It was important to Jesus that his disciples understood that they were having a real encounter with him. Though his resurrection body had different properties than ours, it was still very much a human body of flesh and bone. It could be touched, and it could digest food.

The presence of the marks of crucifixion on Jesus' resurrection body is also problematic for some people.

Do you think we also retain them in the resurrection scars of the wounds we have received on earth?

Our scars are caused by accidents, violence, and medical procedures. They leave permanent reminders of those events on our bodies. The marks of Jesus' crucifixion are the marks that signify the means of redemption. In Heaven, Jesus will be easily recognizable as the only person with scars. These scars will always remain on his resurrection body as a reminder of the grace which gave us our place in God's Heavenly kingdom. Because Jesus retains his scars, our scars will be gone.

Your Body Really is a Temple

1 Corinthians 6:19-20 (NIV)

[19] *Do you not know that your bodies are temples of the Holy Spirit, who is in you, whom you have received from God? You are not your own;* [20] *you were bought at a price. Therefore honor God with your bodies.*

What is a temple, and why is this an appropriate term for the human body?

What is the price Paul speaks about?

Though the Bible says that the decay of our earthly body is inevitable, this should never lead us to neglect our physical nature. Our lives will be happier, and more joyful, if we maintain our bodies well. We sometimes say "Jesus died to save my soul," but this does not mean God is indifferent to the body. We should treat our body as belonging to someone else, because it does!

In what ways is your currently lifestyle contributing to the demise of your body?

Grade yourself on the following aspects of maintaining good health (Choose A B C D F).

___ Avoiding bad habits, like smoking.
___ Maintaining an appropriate weight.
___ Getting adequate rest daily.
___ Getting an appropriate amount of exercise daily.

___ Eating nutritious food.
___ Following through on regular health checkups.
___ Finding healthy ways of coping with stress.

What changes are you willing to make right now to increase the health and functionality of your body?

Choose only one. For example, if you are a fast food junkie, you may want to visit your local grocery store, and discover how to select and prepare real, nutritious food for yourself and your family. Once this has become a permanent part of your lifestyle, you can make another change. With every change, your health and well-being will improve. Your temple will become more glorious. And you will experience more of Heaven on earth!

Doing Justice

Study 6

What should Christians do about the problems of the world?

A. Nothing—leave it to God
B. Pray about them
C. Try to fix things
D. Other

It is important to God that we embrace justice and promote it in our world.

Amos 5:21-24 (NIV)

²¹ *"I hate, I despise your religious festivals;*
your assemblies are a stench to me.
²² *Even though you bring me burnt offerings and grain offerings,*
I will not accept them.
Though you bring choice fellowship offerings,
I will have no regard for them.
²³ *Away with the noise of your songs!*
I will not listen to the music of your harps.
²⁴ *But let justice roll on like a river,*
righteousness like a never-failing stream!

Why is the worship of the Israelites in Amos' day be offensive to God?

Can religious expression alone satisfy God? Why or why not?

Deuteronomy 24:17-19 (NIV)

[17] *Do not deprive the foreigner or the fatherless of justice, or take the cloak of the widow as a pledge.* [18] *Remember that you were slaves in Egypt and the Lord your God redeemed you from there. That is why I command you to do this.*

God's call to justice is connected to what event in Israelite history?

It is common to assume that the Old Testament teaches people to earn God's favor, while the New Testament teaches goodness as our response to God's grace. This is an oversimplification. Even at the time of the giving of the law, the demands of God were justified by the prior mercy of God. Because God gave justice to the enslaved Israelites, God expects his people to give justice to each other. Doing justice is therefore raised beyond duty, and given the status of worship. We do not treat others justly in the hope of gaining favor. We treat others justly because we have already received God's favor.

Now look at the New Testament perspective:

James 2:1-5 (NIV)

My brothers and sisters, believers in our glorious Lord Jesus Christ must not show favoritism. [2] *Suppose a man comes into your meeting wearing a gold ring and fine clothes, and a poor man in filthy old clothes also comes in. ³ If you show special attention to the man wearing fine clothes and say, "Here's a good seat for you," but say to the poor man, "You stand there" or "Sit on the floor by my feet," ⁴ have you not discriminated among yourselves and become judges with evil thoughts?*

⁵ Listen, my dear brothers and sisters: Has not God chosen those who are poor in the eyes of the world to be rich in faith and to inherit the kingdom he promised those who love him?

What would cause Christian people to show favoritism to the wealthy?

Why is such favoritism forbidden in the Church?

Justice is often portrayed in the Bible as being characteristic of a redeemed society. When we see justice, we see the kingdom of God, we have a foretaste of paradise.

What does James mean when he asks, "Has not God chosen the poor of the world . . . ?"

When the Scripture refers to the poor, it often refers to the fact of their powerlessness, rather than their economic status. The poor are powerless and therefore are often the victims of injustice.

Why does the Scripture regard all people as inherently equal?

Who are the greatest victims of injustice today?

What would James say to the Church today? What kinds of favoritism would he criticize?

Look at The Confessing Church as an example of justice.

An "Aryan Paragraph" is a general term for any restriction in a real estate deed that requires that a home be bought or sold by a member of a specific race; a practice which has been outlawed in the USA since the 1940's. It goes back to the practice in Germany from 1887-1945 that required that German national sports-clubs, song societies, school clubs, harvest circles and fraternities to only allow members of the Aryan race.

The Lutheran Church (Evangelical) was the state church in Germany during this dark time. When Aryanism was forced upon the German church by requiring all clergy be of Aryan descent, most local churches went along with it. Their Synod elected an unqualified Nazi puppet named Ludwig Mueller as their Bishop. These "German Christians" soon won 80% of the seats in regional synods, and clergy not embracing the Aryan paragraph were removed from their pulpits.

In response to this outrage, Martin Niemoller began *The Pastor's Emergency League*, the original purpose of which was to care for these pastors who were ousted for political reasons. Eventually, these dissenting pastors met in the city of Barmen to form a distinct church, one faithful to the historic Protestant Confession. They called themselves the *Confessing Church* because they were confessing the true faith, in response to the Nazi false church that was spreading all over Germany. These brave pastors often went to concentration camps and died rather than give to the Aryan program. They often hid Jewish families and helped them to escape Germany illegally. They spoke out against Nazi genocide. A few actively resisted Nazi policies and joined in the Valkyrie attempt to destroy Hitler.

Who do Christians need to stand with today?

What can you do to promote justice in your community?

Study 7

A Sacrifice of Praise

What is your favorite hymn? Why is it your favorite?

Complete the sentence: "I wish worship in our church was more _____."

Romans 12:1-2 (NIV)

12 Therefore, I urge you, brothers and sisters, in view of God's mercy, to offer your bodies as a living sacrifice, holy and pleasing to God—this is your true and proper worship. ² Do not conform to the pattern of this world, but be transformed by the renewing of your mind. Then you will be able to test and approve what God's will is—his good, pleasing and perfect will.

After talking about what Christ has done for us in Chapters 1-11, Paul now begins to talk about how to live in the light of God's grace. He begins by bringing up the idea of **sacrifice**; a central concept of Israelite worship.

The practice of sacrifice is older than history. Archaeological records contain both human and animal corpses with sacrificial marks long which are dated prior to the existence of written records of the practice.

In ancient paganism, literally anything of value could be sacrificed. The more valuable the offering, the more highly the sacrifice is regarded by the Deity. Human or animal lives are deemed the most valuable, but other sacrifices include flowers, candles, incense, spilling some of the drink from a cup before drinking.

How do you suppose the ancient people who practiced extensive sacrifice thought about God?

How is Paul's understanding of sacrifice in Romans 12 distinctive?

A. Who is sacrificed
B. How we sacrifice
C. Why we sacrifice
D. All the above

What is the basis of Paul's appeal?

To appeal by the "mercies of God" reveals a key aspect of Pauline theology and of Christian theology today. God is the initiator of his relationship with us. To Paul, Jesus represents a free act of God, not motivated by anything we do. His death is the supreme act of God's mercy. Therefore anything we do (sacrifice, service and worship) is a response to God's mercy, not a cause of it, as it is in the pagan religions.

Christianity is not a system of beliefs about how to please God and gain his favor. It is a fundamental faith in the favor already given. In other words, we don't worship so God will bless us. We worship because God already has!

How is worship an act of sacrifice?

How is service an act of sacrifice?

What is "spiritual" worship?

The Greek word Paul uses is *logicos,* a surprising word to use and a challenging word to translate. It is not that worship must be logical, rational or reasonable. Logicos refers to that which distinguishes us from animals. Paul is saying that worship; or the ability to reduce ego and live self-consciously outside ourselves is a uniquely human (and therefore a spiritual) capability.

In the natural world, self-sacrifice (altruism) is rare, and is often related to kinship or reciprocity. For example, individual members of certain species of monkey give alarm calls to warn related monkeys of the presence of predators, even though in doing so they attract attention to themselves, increasing their chance of being attacked.

The capacity for self-sacrifice among human beings is much greater than it is among the animals. Soldiers give their lives for their country. Brilliant young people decline lucrative careers in finance and industry to become teachers, police officers, and firefighters. Paul teaches that the ultimate form of worship is to "give oneself" to God. This means living for something greater than ourselves. This form of sacrifice is uniquely human and distinctively spiritual.

Who benefits from worship? The great paradox of worship is that we benefit most by denying ourselves (losing ourselves, sacrificing ourselves, getting outside of ourselves). We are transformed and fully aligned with the will of God. At the same time, we are the most fully human and filled with life. We receive the full blessing of worship when we abandon ourselves completely to the act of giving God praise.

How does this apply to the way people approach worship today as expressed in these popular phrases:

"I go to church for what I can get out of it."
"I go to church because I want to be fed spiritually"

"I need to worship to help me through the week."

"The hymns and prayers are the preliminaries to the sermon."

A March 2007 Gallup Survey indicates that people who attended church were equally divided between those who come seeking guidance and inspiration (43%) and those seeking to worship God (42%). Do you sense the paradox?

Matthew 5:23-24 (NIV)

[23] *"Therefore, if you are offering your gift at the altar and there remember that your brother or sister has something against you,* [24] *leave your gift there in front of the altar. First go and be reconciled to them; then come and offer your gift.*

Rewrite these two verses in your own words:

Why does God care so much about us having good relationships, that he would even tell us to interrupt worship to maintain them?

Who in your church are you having the most trouble getting along with?

How might you reaffirm your love for someone you have not spoken to in a while?

Study **8**

Healing Tears

What was your first experience with death?

Who passed away (for many, their first experience with death was losing a pet)?

How old were you?

How did you react?

How did you start to feel better?

What are the most common reasons people cry today?

When was the last time you cried? What were you crying about?

Psalm 126 (NIV)

A song of ascents.

> [1] *When the Lord restored the fortunes of*[a] *Zion,*
> *we were like those who dreamed.*
> [2] *Our mouths were filled with laughter,*
> *our tongues with songs of joy.*
> *Then it was said among the nations,*
> *"The Lord has done great things for them."*
> [3] *The Lord has done great things for us,*
> *and we are filled with joy.*
>
> [4] *Restore our fortunes, Lord,*
> *like streams in the Negev.*
> [5] *Those who sow with tears*
> *will reap with songs of joy.*
> [6] *Those who go out weeping,*
> *carrying seed to sow,*
> *will return with songs of joy,*
> *carrying sheaves with them.*

A "song of ascents" is most likely a psalm sung or chanted on the way toward Jerusalem. The 15 Songs of Ascents in the book of Psalms may date from the return of the people who came from Israel's southern tribes of Judah and Benjamin. The northern 10 tribes of Israel were conquered in the 8th century BC by the Nation of Assyria. Those tribes were removed from the land, dispersed, and lost. Judah survived the

Assyrian conquest, but was subsequently conquered by the Babylonians in 586 BC. Seventy years later, after Persia conquered Babylonia, the Persian King Cyrus issues the edict that allowed the people of Judah to return to Jerusalem.

Look up *Babylonian Exile* in a Bible Dictionary or Encyclopedia, and learn as much as you can about the exile.

Why God allow the nation to be conquered?

Why were the people taken into exile?

To what do verses 4-6 refer to? What is the Negev?

Do you remember singing (or your parents singing) "Bringing in the Sheaves?"

What are sheaves and why would bringing them in bring joy?

Psalm 126 indicates that we should see crying as the prelude to joy! The arduous work of planting and maintaining crop finally results in a joyful harvest. In the same way, faithful Christian living, even when difficult or painful, ultimately yields a harvest of joy.

At a community hospital in a Chicago suburb, an eight-year-old girl scheduled to have a leg amputated asked, 'May I cry or should I be brave?'" ("Have a Good Cry" by Victor M. Parachin)

Have you ever wanted to ask that question? What did you do . . . cry or act brave?

When you were a child, what did you hear most often when you cried?

- Big boys/girls don't cry.
- If you keep that up, I'll give you something to cry about.
- It's OK to cry.
- Crying never fixed anything.
- Don't be ashamed to cry.
- Other: _____

How did your parents' attitude toward crying influenced how you handle your emotions?

Are you more likely to hold things in or vent?

What are the positive aspects of keeping your emotions to yourself?

What are the positive aspects of venting your emotions?

What are the drawbacks of keeping your emotions to yourself?

What are the drawbacks of venting your emotions?

As far back as 1957, it was known that emotional tears are chemically different from tears that result from eye irritation. Emotional tears contain more beta-endorphins (our body's natural pain relievers), and protein.

According to Dr. William Frey, a biochemist and director of the Dry Eye and Tear Research Center in Minneapolis, Minnesota, one reason people might feel better after crying could be because they are "removing, in their tears, chemicals that build up during emotional stress." Frey's research indicates that tears, along with other bodily secretions like perspiration, rid the body of various toxins and wastes. Tears are one of God's unique ways to wash poison out of our emotions and our bodies.

Are you most likely to cry when you feel:

- Frustrated?
- Grieving?
- Angry?
- Heartbroken?
- Disappointed?
- Other?

Which of the following is the main reason you cry?

- Anxiety 5
- Sadness 49
- Happiness 21
- Fear 5
- Anger 10
- Sympathy 7

Note: The numbers represent the percentages of people who rate each emotion as the most likely moment in which they would cry.

How Christians Handle Emotions

How many times have you not told the truth when someone in church asked you, "How are you?" Why is that so common?

Why can't we be more honest with our brothers and sisters when we are sad?

Do you find it hard to be honest with God about your sadness, fears, hurts, or anger?

Instead of seeing tears as an offense (childish, sign of weakness, over-emotional, embarrassing, etc.) think of tears as the way we empty the soul of sadness to make room for joy.

If you told God how you really felt today, what would you say?

2 Corinthians 1:3-4 (NIV)

3 Praise be to the God and Father of our Lord Jesus Christ, the Father of compassion and the God of all comfort, 4 who comforts us in all our troubles, so that we can comfort those in any trouble with the comfort we ourselves receive from God.

Grief is one of the most common reasons people cry. Grief is an appropriate response to the experience of loss. Bereavement (the loss of a family member or close friend) is only one type of loss which produces grief. What are some other grief-inducing losses?

How have you experienced God's compassion in your life?

Think or describe a time when you felt God comforting you?

What can we do once we have received God's comfort?

Study 9

Done with Sin

Who do you resemble more, your father or your mother?

To what degree have you embraced your parents' faith and values?

Matthew 5:43–48 (NIV)

[43] *"You have heard that it was said, 'Love your neighbor and hate your enemy.'* [44] *But I tell you, love your enemies and pray for those who persecute you,* [45] *that you may be children of your Father in Heaven. He causes his sun to rise on the evil and the good, and sends rain on the righteous and the unrighteous.* [46] *If you love those who love you, what reward will you get? Are not even the tax collectors doing that?* [47] *And if you greet only your own people, what are you doing more than others? Do not even pagans do that?* [48] *Be perfect, therefore, as your Heavenly Father is perfect.*

How do you react to Jesus' call that we be perfect?

A. Yeah, right.
B. I'm already perfect, can't you see?

C. I give up, just turn on the TV
D. I'll try my hardest to be perfect.
E. I can't, but God can.

The correct response is E. The Christian life is a life lived in response to God's grace.

Write a definition of grace:

Grace is sometimes described with the word *prevenient* (pre=before; venire = Latin to come or to go). Prevenient grace refers to the fact that God loves us before we love God. Do you see prevenient Grace in Matt 5:43–48?

Who gets sunshine in God's world?

Grace is also involved in the moment *Justification*. When we decide to accept the Love of God, our sins our washed away, and we begin a personal relationship with God. Justification is a result of our acceptance of the grace offered through Jesus Christ.

Grace is also involved in the process of *Sanctification*. We are not instantly perfected, but continue to grow in a process of life-long transformation, with the goal that we would someday love others as God loves them. Sanctification is understood to be the work of the Holy Spirit.

Some Christians believe in *Entire Sanctification*. This occurs when the work of the Holy Spirit is complete. It is also known as *Christian perfection*.

Do you think entire sanctification is possible in this life?

In Matthew 5, Jesus it telling us what perfection looks like. He is showing us where the target is.

It is interesting that the Greek word for "sin," *hamartia* ("ha" = no, martia = military skill), literally means to "miss the mark."

The old hymn *Rock of Ages* contains these words: "Be of sin the double-cure . . ." Why does sin require a "double" cure?

Sin creates a problem of g_____ before God.
Sin becomes deeply rooted in us and c_____ us.

So says the hymn: ". . . Save me from its guilt and power."

Jesus resolves the "double problem" (legal and personal) we have with sin. He removed the moral guilt and enables us to have a relationship with God. He then gives the Holy Spirit to sanctify us and helps us be more "godly."

A fine way of visualizing the process of sanctification was given by Discipleship Movement leader Bob Mumford in his 1976 book, *The King and You* (Baker Books, 1976.). He describes how the Holy Spirit works to realign our will to God's will:

This line represents the steady, unchanging will of God:

━━

This line represents Jesus' will: *"I always do the things that please him"*—John 8:29.

━━

The human will: "I do the things that please God, when it pleases me!"

As sanctification takes place, the Holy Spirit works in us, roots out sin, and helps our will to line up with God's will:

In what ways has your will changed to become more aligned with the will of God?

How can you tell you are being sanctified?

Discuss or think about these evidences of the process of sanctification:

- You learn you don't need to be right all the time.
- You don't need to dominate others.
- You don't need to be superior.
- You accept others the way you find them, not the way you want them.
- You can put other's needs before your own.
- You see others as God sees them.
- You return to reliance on God

To be perfect, in the context of Jesus' Sermon on the Mount, means something close to "accurately embodying God's love in the world."

We should even love our enemies because God loves them. The evidence for his love is that God gives all people what they need: sunshine and rain.

Being "perfect" means not settling for the typical expectations regarding human relationships, that we would love our friends and hate our enemies. We should be more than good enough, we should take after our gracious Father, who loves all.

Do you believe God loves everyone?

Who do you find it difficult to love?

What can you do to change?

Study 10
God in Our World

John 1:15-18 (NIV)

15 (John testified concerning him. He cried out, saying, "This is the one I spoke about when I said, 'He who comes after me has surpassed me because he was before me.'") 16 Out of his fullness we have all received grace in place of grace already given. 17 For the law was given through Moses; grace and truth came through Jesus Christ. 18 No one has ever seen God, but the one and only Son, who is himself God and is in closest relationship with the Father, has made him known.

In what way did Jesus come "after" John the Baptist?

In what way did Jesus come "before" John the Baptist?

If we are all God's children, why do we speak about Jesus as "God's one and only Son"?

The Bible tells us that no one has ever seen God (John 1:18) except the Jesus Christ the divine Son. In Exodus 33:20, God declares, "You cannot see my face, for no one may see me and live." These Scriptures seem to conflict with other Scriptures which describe various people "seeing" God. For example, Exodus 33:19-23 describes Moses speaking to God "face to face." How could Moses speak with God "face to face" if no one can see God's face and live (Choose the best answer below)?

    A. "Face to face" is a figure of speech indicating a unique level of intimacy.
    B. The Bible says contradictory things all the time
    C. Moses said this to validate his own authority

The best answer is A. Moses had a unique level of intimacy with God. God chose Moses to be the one through whom he would deliver his people from slavery, and the one who would lead the people in developing their unique identity as God's people. God spoke directly to Moses, and Moses conveyed God's laws to the people. So in this regard, the expression "face to face" refers to direct communication between God and his servant.

In what way did Jesus "see" God that we cannot?

John 14:8-10 (NIV)

[8] *Philip said, "Lord, show us the Father and that will be enough for us."*
[9] *Jesus answered: "Don't you know me, Philip, even after I have been among you such a long time? Anyone who has seen me has seen the Father. How can you say, 'Show us the Father'?* [10] *Don't you believe that I am in the Father, and that the Father is in me? The words I say to you I do not speak on my own authority. Rather, it is the Father, living in me, who is doing his work.*

What was Philip's request? How does Jesus answer it?

How do we see God in Jesus?

What does Jesus reveal to us about God?

We need to be careful with people who claim to have seen God or Jesus face to face. We do not need to be critical, just wise. We need to ask ourselves, is the God this person claims to have seen the same God Jesus revealed to us?

1 Peter 1:6-9 (NIV)

[6] *In all this you greatly rejoice, though now for a little while you may have had to suffer grief in all kinds of trials.* [7] *These have come so that the proven genuineness of your faith—of greater worth than gold, which perishes even though refined by fire—may result in praise, glory and honor when Jesus Christ is revealed.* [8] *Though you have not seen him, you love him; and even though you do not see him now, you believe in him and are filled with an inexpressible and glorious joy,* [9] *for you are receiving the end result of your faith, the salvation of your souls.*

If you saw God in person today, how would that effect your faith?

Peter talks about how blessed it is when people are faithful to God without the benefit of a direct experience of God. Do you have to see God to believe in him?

If people saw God, would they be better able to believe?

On earth, our experience of God is most likely to be indirect. Where do you most often see God?

A. Nature
B. Other people
C. Church
D. Miracles
E. The Mirror
F. Somewhere else

In Heaven, we will have a face-to-face experience of God's presence. To have Heaven on earth, we need to "see" God in our daily lives. This means:

1. Being more aware of his presence.
2. Being more grateful for his care.
3. Watching for everyday miracles.
4. Keeping alert to the opportunities God gives us.

Behold! God is right there.

The biblical word *behold* is a word that invites us to look; to pay attention to what God is doing. It appears 1,298 times in the King James Version of the Bible. It is the traditional word used to translate the Hebrew word *hinneh* and the Greek word *idou*. Contemporary translations of the Bible avoid using *behold* and often choose instead the word "look." But *beholding* is much more than looking.

The word *behold* also often serves as a marker in the biblical text. When you read the word behold, you are seeing a word that is saying "pay attention to what comes next! This is important!" There is no English word that has the same power or weight.

The word behold is the word that tells us God has something he really wants us to see. Note the use of *behold* in these passages, cited in the KJV:

Behold, a virgin shall be with child, and shall bring forth a son, and they shall call his name Emmanuel, which being interpreted is, God with us. (Matthew 1:23)

Often the word *behold* alerts us that we are about to hear something shocking or surprising; something that goes against our normal understanding of things. Behold is the word that invites us to look for thing difficult to see in a casual glance. A passage of particular interest is found in Luke 17:20-21.

And when he was demanded of the Pharisees, when the kingdom of God should come, he answered them and said, The kingdom of God cometh not with observation: Neither shall they say, Lo here! or, lo there! for, behold, the kingdom of God is within you.

I appreciate that Bible scholars say that it's difficult to determine from the formation of the original biblical language whether Jesus meant inside of us, among us, or within our grasp. But his point was that when we are talking about the Kingdom of God we don't have to go out looking for it. The Kingdom of God is right there.

One essential skill we all need to experience Heaven on earth is the skill of *beholding*. Our culture's commitment to the proverb "seeing is believing," is our greatest obstacle to seeing the presence of God who is all around us, within us, and right there for us. If fact, the opposite is even more true.

It is the act of believing that enables us to see.

Study 11

Living into Eternal Life

1 Corinthians 5:1-4

For we know that if the earthly tent we live in is destroyed, we have a building from God, an eternal house in heaven, not built by human hands. [2] Meanwhile we groan, longing to be clothed instead with our heavenly dwelling, [3] because when we are clothed, we will not be found naked. [4] For while we are in this tent, we groan and are burdened, because we do not wish to be unclothed but to be clothed instead with our heavenly dwelling, so that what is mortal may be swallowed up by life.

To what kind of structure does Paul compare our earthly bodies?

To what kind of structure does Paul compare our heavenly bodies?

What are some differences between a tent and a house?

A tent is a type of home that serves a temporary purpose. What does that say about our earthly lives?

Philippians 1:21-25

[21] *For to me, to live is Christ and to die is gain.* [22] *If I am to go on living in the body, this will mean fruitful labor for me. Yet what shall I choose? I do not know!* [23] *I am torn between the two: I desire to depart and be with Christ, which is better by far;* [24] *but it is more necessary for you that I remain in the body.* [25] *Convinced of this, I know that I will remain, and I will continue with all of you for your progress and joy in the faith,*

Paul's awareness of the possibility of his death while imprisoned for his faith, led to consideration of his purpose.

Which did Paul think was better for him personally, dying or living on?

Why did Paul think it was better overall for him to continue to live?

John Wesley, the founder of the Methodist movement, grew up in Epworth, England, where his father Samuel was pastor. On February 9, 1709, a fire broke out in the rectory. All of the Wesley children escaped quickly, except for five year old John, who was trapped on the second floor. He was rescued by neighbors, who formed a human ladder to reach the upper story window. Later in life, John Wesley referred to himself as a "brand plucked from the burning." This expression alludes to Zechariah 3:2 and Amos 4:11. It indicates that Wesley saw himself as having been saved for a special purpose.

Think about a time when you had a close "brush with death." What happened?

How did that close brush with death change you?

List one or more possible reasons you have not gone to Heaven yet.

The brush with death experience only amplifies what should be our awareness every day. We are all mortal beings, who live only a short time on earth. We are living in a tent, temporarily on earth to serve God until he calls us to our home in Heaven.

Preparedness for the Journey

Write down the top 5 things you are proud of in your life.

1.
2.
3.
4.
5.

Write a note to God below, thanking him for enabling you to have or do these things.

Write down the top 5 things you regret about your life.

1.

2.

3.

4.

5.

Write a note to God seeking forgiveness for these things.

Write down the things you appreciate most about every member of your immediate family.

Spouse:

Child 1:

Child 2:

Child 3:

Other:

Now, in a way that would be comfortable for both of you, communicate to them what you wrote.

Fill out this Checklist

___ Do you trust Jesus?
___ Have you made out your will?
___ Do you have a Living Will or Advance Directives?
___ Have you made a choice about organ donation?
___ Do you have adequate Life Insurance?

___ Have you planned and paid for your funeral?

___ Have you written down your preferences (Scriptures, Music, etc.) for your Funeral or Memorial Service?

___ Have you designated someone to be your power of attorney?

___ Have you designated someone to be your health care representative or surrogate?

___ Have you designated a guardian to care for your children if they are still young when you die?

___ If you have a special needs child, have you consulted with a professional (such as a medical social worker) who can help you understand Medicare and Medicaid rules and do special needs planning?

The more complete your preparations are, the more serenity you will feel, and the less you will have to think about the end of life. Preparing for death helps us focus on living!

Ecclesiastes 11:7-8

Light is sweet,
and it pleases the eyes to see the sun.
⁸ However many years anyone may live,
let them enjoy them all.
But let them remember the days of darkness,
for there will be many.
Everything to come is meaningless.

What one thing can you do more of so that you might experience the "sweetness" of life in a greater way?

Write down the name of a person you need to forgive.

Write down the name of someone from whom you should seek forgiveness.

When Solomon says "Everything is meaningless" he is saying that, in the end, nothing we achieve or accomplish in life lasts for eternity. God does not admit us to Heaven because of what we have accomplished. On what basis does God admit us to Heaven?

If we trust in our own goodness to get us into heaven, we can have hope. If we trust in God's goodness, we can have assurance.

In whom do you put your trust?

CPSIA information can be obtained
at www.ICGtesting.com
Printed in the USA
FFOW02n0626290814
7133FF